STRATEGIES OF

CURRICULUM DEVELOPMENT

Virgil E. Herrick

STRATEGIES OF

CURRICULUM DEVELOPMENT

The works of
VIRGIL E. HERRICK
compiled by   *Dan W. Andersen*
James B. Macdonald
Frank B. May

GREENWOOD PRESS, PUBLISHERS
WESTPORT, CONNECTICUT

Library of Congress Cataloging in Publication Data
Herrick, Virgil E
    Strategies of curriculum development.

    Reprint of the ed. published by C. E. Merrill,
Columbus, Ohio.
    Bibliography of Herrick's works: p.
    Includes bibliographical references.
    1. Curriculum development. I. Title.
[LB1570.H47 1975]   375'.001   74-1781
ISBN 0-8371-7400-7

Originally published in 1965 by Charles E. Merrill Books, Inc.,
Columbus, Ohio.

Reprinted with the permission of Charles E. Merrill Publishing
Company.

Reprinted in 1975 by Greenwood Press,
A division of Congressional Information Service, Inc.
88 Post Road West, Westport, Connecticut 06881

Library of Congress catalog card number 74-1781
ISBN 0-8371-7400-7

Printed in the United States of America

10 9 8 7 6 5 4 3 2

Preface

Curriculum theory has often been based in the past on a large body of implicit and inconsistent assumptions. It is presently emerging as a field of inquiry based on rational and coherent propositions. As a field, it is beginning to attract enough followers to produce generous returns in our understanding of curriculum problems and processes.

This book is composed of the edited works of the late Virgil E. Herrick, who, early in his professional career, recognized the need for disciplined curriculum theory and who devoted a sizable portion of his professional labor to the exploration and development of this discipline.

This book includes some previously published articles (which have been slightly edited in some instances), but primarily of previously unpublished papers. These materials have stood the test of time, criticism of colleagues, and critiques by graduate students in curriculum seminars. Although the ideas of Professor Herrick are based partially on those of other educational leaders, a large degree of originality will be evident to readers of this volume. Many of his ideas were nurtured and refined by his colleagues and students at Syracuse University, The University of

Chicago, The University of Wisconsin, and other institutions with which he came in contact.

The editors wish both to commemorate a deeply respected and loved mentor who made an indelible impression upon their lives, and also to present to curriculum theorists and practitioners the fruits of many years of work, which have resulted in a significant presentation of ideas relevant to curriculum development.

The journey is not finished. We are a long way from a definitive curriculum theory. Professor Herrick was always willing to admit this fact and to encourage others to reach beyond his concepts.

It is sometimes difficult to separate the impact of ideas from the impact of the man who presents them. Dr. Herrick was a man with a forceful personality, and the ideas he expressed tended to gain force from his own intensity, conviction, and depth of insight. This was particularly true in the area of curriculum theory, in which our court of last appeal is frequently not the process of empirical validation. Yet, without this conviction and depth of insight, Dr. Herrick would undoubtedly have given up this field of inquiry as a waste of time many years ago. Nevertheless, in the long run, the ideas which are set forth in this volume will stand or fall on their own merit, as Dr. Herrick would have wanted them to.

Virgil Herrick believed in cutting through the shell of specific instances and revealing the underlying assumptions. His work reflects this approach in its continuous retracing of logic and form back of the basic referents of curriculum—society, the learner, and man's knowledge. Regardless of topic or aspect of curriculum, there is evident in his work the tendency to begin with these referents as a base and to move toward clarification and solution of problems.

Professor Herrick believed that man is essentially rational and therefore able to discipline his intelligence and use it for a rational selection among the alternative solutions to a problem. This basic value commitment should be evident in this volume. Another value commitment was evident in his desire to move toward a descriptive theory of curriculum—one which isolated and defined the basic curricular components and their relationships. In this sense he shared the commitment of all scientists toward description, explanation, and control of phenomena.

There is a cumulative impact in the ideas expressed in this volume which the editors felt was not obtainable through a perusal of single papers or articles. This impact comes through in the form of a theoretical framework, powerful in nature, set to work on a series of topics or problems. This framework revolves around the basic referents of curriculum, and around the teaching operations and their patterns of interaction. Further, there is a consistent and over-riding conviction which stands as a theme throughout the volume—that analysis of the teaching operations should be central to the development of curricular and instructional theory and practice and that research and theorizing which disregard the central operations of teaching are doomed to early extinction despite their popularity.

Those convictions and ideas permeate the three major interests of Professor Herrick—the evolution of curriculum theory and design, the improvement of instructional theory and practice, and the analysis of classroom episodes as a method of inquiry for testing ideas about curriculum design and instructional theory. These three interests are represented by the three sections of this book.

The editors would be remiss not to emphasize their own fallibility. We may well have selected papers and articles which, to other colleagues or students of Professor Herrick, do not adequately represent the quality and significance of his ideas. It is also possible that as the result of joining the ideas of several papers or deleting certain ideas from other papers we have done some damage. Our personal biases and editorial mistakes are largely unavoidable. We can only reiterate that our intent has been to honor a great man and to provide others with the opportunity of beginning or renewing an acquaintance with his ideas.

D. W. A.

J. B. M.

F. B. M.

Table of Contents

PART ONE

Developing
Curriculum-design Theory

*What are some of the problems on which cur-
riculum theorists need to focus their attention?*

*What are the effects on curriculum design of
focusing on one referent rather than another: subject
matter, society, or learner?*

*What influences will the various philosophical
and empirical studies presently underway have on
curriculum design?*

*Part I is devoted to statements about curriculum
theory and design. The first selection relates the
need for curriculum theory and design and the
various problems which must be considered in
developing them. This selection is followed by a
statement regarding the components of curriculum
design and the relationships between these components which need to be established. The third
selection is a description of one design—the experience curriculum—and the last selection in Part I
is a projection of a variety of avenues for growth
and development in the field of curriculum.*

D. W. A.
J. B. M.
F. B. M.

1

Problems of the Curriculum Theorist*

The problems on which curriculum theorists need to focus their attention, and the problem of defining the discipline of curriculum theory are placed in perspective by noting the difficulties encountered in defining any theoretical discipline. More serious problems are then delineated, and directions toward solutions are suggested.

D. W. A.
J. B. M.
F. B. M.

Students of the curriculum and its related problems of instructional methodology do not share a precise definition of *curriculum*, nor do they agree on the nature of the observations to be made or the range of phenomena which are to be incorporated into curriculum planning or theorizing. Many illustrations can be found of individuals who see curriculum in a very limited fashion, whereas others see it so broadly that curriculum becomes synonymous with life itself. Both views may be equally invalid.

This problem is shared, however, with all scholars of complex, dynamic, physical, biological, and social phenomena. The dilemma

---

* The original source of this selection and of all other selections is noted in the Credits on p. 185.

of the sociologist in dealing with the concept of a community, the difficulties of the psychologist and psychiatrist with the problems of human personality, and the struggling of the philosopher with the various questions of knowing—all represent problems comparable to our own.

We realize that the discipline of history, for example, becomes meaningful only when it is attached to some object, person, geographical area, social institution, or political unit. Thus we have the history of the steam engine, of George Washington, of the arctic region, of the school, or of the United States. This history is further specialized by the use of such terms as "social," "political," "educational," "economic," or "biographical."

The difficulty of knowing what to consider, the nature of the approach, and the appropriate method of inquiry to use can be illustrated in almost any field of study. Therefore, although one might talk a great deal about studying chemistry as chemistry, the clarity and specificity of this referent becomes less obvious when one attempts to discover what chemistry, what structure, and what intellectual discipline one is talking about. Perhaps the stability and clarity of the unique structure of a given body of knowledge is more obvious to the observer if he is looking at the products of a hundred years of trying to build nice, logically consistent compartments and distinctions than it would be if he were looking at the fresh, green, growing edge of its field of inquiry.

ESTABLISHING PRIORITIES

There are only three basic referents or orientations possible to consider in the development of distinctive curriculum patterns and in making many pivotal curriculum decisions. These three referents are (1) man's categorized and preserved knowledge—the subject fields; (2) our society, its institutions and social processes; and (3) the individual to be educated, his nature, needs, and developmental patterns. These three referents are the sources from which curriculum development and theorizing spring. They are also the source for the ancient controversies over the subject-centered, social-centered, and individual-centered curriculums. Many of our problems of curriculum analyzing and development come from either a refusal to realize that all of these referents are a necessary part of the analysis or an unwillingness to face up to the major question of the initial and basic priority of one of these referents over the others in building a curriculum design.

There can be only three fundamentally different approaches to curriculum planning. The traditional curriculum pattern in our schools has encompassed *organized subject matter* and its conventional categories; less frequently has a *social framework* of our society or the emergent developmental patterns of the *individual* been used. These three characteristic curriculum patterns do not differ in the sense that each pattern's over-all purpose or function is different or that different components are considered. A curriculum pattern differs from the others only in the priority and order of the referents used to develop the specifics of a given instructional program

The problem of curriculum development, therefore, is never the consideration of a single source for the development, but the more complicated question of considering the initial priority and order of the three fundamental considerations of all thinking concerning curriculum and instruction. Each curriculum program will consider at some point the individual, the concerns of the society in which he exists, and the significant ideas and intellectual processes of man's experience and cultural heritage. The curriculum decision which is difficult is to determine how these necessary components can be arranged in a given curriculum structure so as to deal most effectively with the complex educational problems of the present and future. Any proposal for improvement of curriculum, therefore, cannot find hope for an adequate solution to the problems by advocating that any one of these basic referents will hold all the necessary answers.

This oversimplified examination of the components of curriculum and their characteristic patterning can be used to point up many of our present dilemmas in curriculum development. Each of the characteristic approaches to curriculum planning and instruction is supported by a particular concept of the function and role of the school in our American culture, a particular philosophic concept of knowing and knowledge, a specific way of looking at learning and its conditions, and a set of specialized convictions as to the particular role and responsibilities of the teacher and learner.

A preoccupation with subject fields leads directly to problems of generalizing, the cognitive processes, the logical structures of subject matter, transfer of training, mental discipline, readiness, repetition, motivation, reinforcement, retention, and the ability of the individual to learn. A preoccupation with a socially centered curriculum leads to the examination of the nature of persistent and recurring social problems, social and democratic processes, group dynamics, valuing and normative behavior, organismic and topological concepts of learning, and status- and role-determining processes. A preoccupation with the learner as the initial consideration in curriculum building leads to examination of the self-perceptive process, the mechanisms for the identification of persistent and recurring concerns of the individual, questions of creativity, phenomenological fields, biological growth processes, and what constitutes maturity and development in the human organism.

MAKING VALUE DECISIONS

This brief examination of the basic referents in curriculum suggests the following conclusions about curriculum development:

1. In curriculum planning and development, we cannot escape the value decision concerning the initial and basic orientation of the curriculum structure we are creating. This decision is not made on the evidence provided by a contributing discipline, yet it directs and in part defines the learning theory, the kinds of social analyses, and the role definitions for the teachers and students. In each of the supporting disciplines of curriculum, it is possible to find points of view and contributions which support any approach to curriculum now known.

2. We have not faced up to the problem of the relationship that should exist between a conceived curriculum structure, which identifies the nature of the contributions of the supporting disciplines, and the consideration of new knowledge in these areas, which suggests new curriculum patterns. The responsibility for dealing with this dilemma rests fundamentally with those who work on problems of curriculum theory and structure, and not with those who are preoccupied with its separate aspects or with the scholars in various fields of knowledge.

3. We have not reconciled the fact that although the over-all goals of curriculum thinking are primarily social and personal, the prevailing curriculum orientation is to subject matter. To what extent should the basic referent for curriculum structure be consistent with our important goals? This value-means dilemma grows fundamentally out of the fact that our means are frequently dictated by factors other than our professed values.

The present demand for more scientists, mathematicians, and for people who speak more than one language, for example, pressures our schools' curriculum into more science, mathematics, and language instruction and thus into a curriculum with subject matter as a basic orientation. Yet the present concern for creative intelligence, for independent and imaginative thinking, for ways to deal with social issues, and for personal and social values seems to push the curriculum worker toward different orientations. From the point of view of curriculum planning we have only four alternatives: (a) to bring these latter aspects to the subject matter framework, (b) to bring subject matter to a social or personal framework, (c) to allocate these two kinds of concerns to different aspects of the curriculum, (d) to assign the responsibility for development to other educational agencies.

ELIMINATING DICHOTOMY BETWEEN CONTENT AND PROCESS

Another area of confusion in curriculum thinking is the conflict that seems to exist between content and process as necessary aspects of curriculum and instruction. Given any object, topic, or area of study, it is possible for one to gain information about it while at the same time learning ways to deal with the topic and to verify the information gained. Students of subject matter in particular content fields always point out that besides the substantive content of a respective field there is always a corresponding intellectual discipline, a way of thinking about and using the data of that field.

The major point for curriculum thinking is that in the development of any adequate teaching-learning situation, there are always two kinds of related objectives—objectives of content and those of process. Any given experience with the learner always achieves multiple objectives that are related in the sense that they must include both ideas *and* process.

Simple propositions, therefore, about the fact that "It does not make very much difference how schools and teachers do it so long as children know certain facts and are able to practice certain skills" are as much in error as contrasting statements to the effect that "It does not make very much difference what you teach, it is the way you teach that makes the important difference." What we know about curriculum and learning suggests that education must deal with important ideas in important ways; both are necessary and critical aspects of any adequately conceived education. If the learner is to gain competency in understanding processes as well as learning them, then the teaching methods and instructional practices used to achieve these two components must use them as one of the bases for determining the practices to be followed.

The problem of content should be a fruitful area of research and study in curriculum. The problems in this area range in one direction to the philosophical deliberations concerning what constitutes knowledge and in the other to the communication problem of trying to cut down the twenty-year lag in getting well-documented and authenticated subject matter into the curriculum. There is no question but that in the last thirty years of curriculum development, greater attention has been given to the study of child development and to the social scene than has been given to the nature of subject matter and its selection and organization for instructional purposes.

CLARIFYING THE NATURE OF PROCESSES

It is possible to identify four process areas which are relatively common to all instructional fields and which should be considered in any curriculum approach. These process or ability areas include: (1) the *language processes* related to the communication and the clarification of understandings, personal and social roles, and valuing operations; (2) the *thought processes* which have to do with verifying and validating data, generalizing, inferring and predicting consequences (perceptive and creative thinking are included here); (3) the *social processes* through which self-concepts are progressively clarified and effective interpersonal relationships and actions are promoted; (4) the *abilities* which are involved in the selection and effective use of educational tools and resources—people, books, dictionaries, maps, charts, globes, and the like. Without regard to how the curriculum planning is done, conscious attention must be paid to how increasing maturity in each of these four process areas is gained by the learner.

Although it is impossible here to document what is being done in each of the above process areas, a brief mention should be made of the work that is being done in the area of language process. In addition to the interesting attacks being made on the structure and nature of the language arts, Louis Raths has looked at the language processes of the teacher as a part of his clarifying, exploring, supporting, and security giving functions. Dwayne Huebner [1] has examined the communication process in his attempt to develop an adequate theory of classroom action. B. Othaniel Smith [2] uses the language patterns of teachers and pupils in his study of the logical patterns in classroom behavior. His 1960 book [3] further portrays the problem of using language in dealing with the major concepts of education itself. These efforts to study language and its processes in the teaching-learning act are suggestive of future developments in this area. The importance of the implications of these studies for curriculum development seems clear.

CLARIFYING THE ROLE OF VALUES IN CURRICULUM DEVELOPMENT

It is obvious that every experience for an individual has some kind of importance, some kind of breadth or scope, some kind of organization, and some kind of extension in time. It is not necessary to have schools or to worry about curriculum development in order

---

[1] Dwayne Huebner, *From Classroom Actions to Educational Outcomes; An Exploration in Education Theory,* unpublished Ph.D. thesis (Madison, Wisconsin: Department of Education, University of Wisconsin, 1959) 212 pp.

[2] B. Othanel Smith et al., *A Study of the Logic of Teaching* (Urbana, Illinois: Bureau of Education Research, University of Illinois, 1960) 115 pp.

[3] ———————— and Robert A. Ennis, *Language and Concepts in Education* (Chicago: Rand McNally & Co., 1961) 221 pp.

for this to be true. The important value decisions of curriculum, however, have to do with the difficult question of what constitutes the educational significance of an experience or its adequacy in respect to scope, organization, and continuity. These questions fundamentally concern the relative potential of alternative experiences to meet a set of certain characteristics. There is seldom one perfect answer. All approaches to curriculum planning and development involve choices of this nature, but each uses a different set of values for determining what constitutes adequacy or significance. An important contribution to curriculum development would be to identify and make clear the value referents for making the important curriculum choices.

It is suggested that:

1. Since any significant, purposeful behavior on the part of a human being will always involve intellectual, emotional, and value components, it seems impossible to have programs of "intellectual education," "emotional education," or "value education."

2. Although greatest attention has been paid to the cognitive aspects of learning, increased attention should be paid to the dimensions of feeling and value. Carl Rogers, in his studies of counseling, for example, recognized the feelings of the individual to be of first importance in the clarification of an understanding of oneself and the world. Philosophers have always concerned themselves with the value questions of life and behavior, seeing them as powerful conveyors of education. Workers in child-study programs [4,5] and in programs of in-service teacher education [6] recognize that any significant long-term change in educational orientation and behavior comes as the result of changes in value and not as a result of accumulated information.

---

[4] Orville G. Brim, Jr., "Recent Research on Effects of Education in Human Development," Chap. LV in *Four Basic Aspects of Preventive Psychiatry*, Report on the First Institute on Preventive Psychiatry, Ralph H. Ozemann, ed. (Iowa City, Iowa: State University of Iowa, 1957) pp. 60–88.

[5] Daniel A. Prescott, *The Child In the Educative Process* (New York: McGraw-Hill Book Company, 1957) pp. 410–69.

[6] National Society for the Study of Education, "Inservice Education of Teachers, Supervisors, and Administrators," Fifty-sixth Yearbook, Part 1 (Chicago: University of Chicago Press, 1957).

3. We have a growing body of evidence to show that the same principles of "set" development, personality integration, and psychotherapy may be used either positively or negatively to turn out passive followers or independent citizens; to build personality or to destroy it; to develop individuals who are passive, rigid, unsure, and authoritarian, as well as individuals who are confident, open, sincere, independent, and spontaneous. Our growing knowledge in the behavioral sciences about the control and prediction of human behavior presents the educators and the curriculum builders with a demanding array of choices.

4. We need more empirical studies like Carroll's,[7] which examined intensively a one year's sample of the *verbal valuing statements* of two groups of teachers. Verbal valuing statements are those which are used to justify or to reinforce the significance of the learning activities of children. Carroll found that there was high agreement among teachers' valuing, pupils' valuing, and the pupils' explanation of teacher valuing in the area of social relationships. There was little agreement among these judgments with respect to the areas of ways of working on learning problems and of ways to deal with a specific classroom situation.

5. We need to develop teaching programs which consciously relate the valuing operations to the learning experiences children have in school. The experimental testing of contrasting approaches to the same value system would be exciting.

The point of the above discussion for curriculum is clear: if we want quality in education programs, and creativity, imagination, independence, resourcefulness, and problem-solving ability to be considered important values, then our educational practices must support, reflect, and encourage these virtues. Because values involve choices and because problem solving involves problems to solve, educational programs which include these factors must pay conscious attention to emotions and valuing operations as well as to intelligence and ideas. These are not contradictory components of learning; they are necessary and supporting aspects of all purposive and differentiating human behavior.

---

[7] Margaret Carroll, *Verbal Valuing in Elementary School Classroom,* unpublished Ph.D. thesis (Madison, Wisconsin: The University of Wisconsin, 1954) p. 300.

CLARIFYING THE NATURE OF
CURRICULUM OPERATIONS

The curriculum operations concerned with determining goals, with selecting learning experiences appropriate to these goals, with organizing and developing these experiences, with evaluating, and with planning are useful reference points for theorization and development in curriculum. These operations serve as reference points for the contributions of philosophers, psychologists, and sociologists as well as subject specialists. Because they are common to all curriculum thinking and planning, and because they are neutral with respect to value, they can be used to compare and differentiate the thinking in various curriculum approaches.

The central operational problem of curriculum to which all others make their contribution is in organization and development. All curriculum planning centers on this operation. The organization of anything includes three necessary aspects: (1) the identification of the parts or aspects to be organized; (2) the identification of the organizing foci for relating the parts; (3) a pattern of relationships or a structure within which relationships can be seen and new patterns can evolve. Because classroom behavior and learning is always social, dynamic, and developmental, the question of what constitutes an effective organizing center—for relating ideas, processes, feelings, people, and problem areas and for providing a vehicle for the necessary extensions in generalization, time, geography, culture, and self-perception—is a critical area in curriculum theory.

It is proposed, therefore, that a careful, systematic examination of the essential aspects of each operational area in curriculum will provide a map of the curriculum domain and a means for revealing the tasks of curriculum study and research.

DEVELOPING WAYS OF STUDYING
CURRICULUM STRUCTURE

Enough has been said, thus far, to point out that one needs to have some concept of what the important components of curriculum are and how these components of curriculum relate in order to form a meaningful whole. Virtually everyone accepts this general point of view, but most find it difficult to make much progress in dealing with the general problem of structure or design. It is possible, however, to make some very modest suggestions as to possible methods of approaching this problem.

1. Present available approaches should be compared and contrasted as to how they deal with common curriculum operations. This kind of study reveals the structure of relationships among the answers to these questions, and it also permits exploration of the assumptions and values upon which such answers are based. Out of this exploration comes a sense of the strength and of the gaps in our present curriculum thinking, a feeling for aspects of curriculum not based on very meaningful evidence, and some conviction as to where one wishes to make his own research effort.

2. A study of the curricular structures of varying subject fields should be made.

A study of the design or structure of a subject field which could make teaching and learning in that field meaningful and significant would have much to offer to a study of curriculum design.

3. The study of curriculum from the points of view of the roles of individuals involved in its operations would be essential.

Curriculum is always, from one point of view, a social system, including a teacher and students as its central focus, with the social structure and personnel of the school and community contributing to it. From this point of view, school learning comes as the result of human interaction taking place in the physical, social, and emotional environment of the school. One profitable way of approaching the study of curriculum, therefore, would be to make an analysis of the roles played by teachers and students in teaching-learning situations. Our recent studies of perception in the learning process and in social behavior, and the present emphasis on self-discovery and realization are all tied to the behavior of teachers and children.

The exploratory study by Gross, Mason, and McEachern [8] of the role of the school superintendency has much to suggest for

---

[8] Neal Gross, Ward B. Mason, and Alexander W. McEachern, *Explorations in Role Analysis* (New York: John Wiley & Sons, Inc., 1958) p. 379.

this kind of analysis in curriculum. Nerbovig [9] used a form of this approach to examine the ways in which teachers use objectives, an attack which seemed to prove fruitful.

4. The study of curriculum structure from the point of view of various theoretical models is another factor.

Parsons and Shils' [10] theory of social action has been used as a framework for analyzing curriculum structures. Macdonald's [11] study showed that, although nomenclature is a real barrier to analysis of a system in different fields, the concepts of boundaries, characteristics of equilibrium, the force dimensions of action space, and the force phases of action movement were helpful in suggesting aspects of social theory which have some relevancy to curriculum theory. His major contribution was the underscoring of the significance of the patterning of decisions about the various questions of curriculum and the concept of the organizing center as a basis for dealing with action space and action movement problems in instruction. It is likely that systematic study of any comprehensive theory of learning, or of personality, would be equally valuable.

5. The study of curriculum structure from the point of view of classroom interaction is necessary.

The work of Flanders, [12] Huebner, [13] Smith, [14] Wright and

---

[9] Marcella Nerbovig, *Teachers' Perception of the Functions of Objectives*, unpublished Ph.D. thesis (Madison, Wisconsin: Department of Education, University of Wisconsin, 1956).

[10] T. Parsons and E. A. Shils, *Toward a General Theory of Action* (Cambridge, Mass.: Harvard University Press, 1952).

T. Parsons, R. F. Bales, and E. A. Shils, *Working Papers in the Theory of Action* (New York: Free Press of Glencoe, Inc., 1953).

T. Parsons, *Family, Socialization, and Interaction Processes* (New York: Free Press of Glencoe, Inc., 1955).

[11] James Bradley Macdonald, *Some Contributions of a General Behavioral Theory for Curriculum*, unpublished Ph.D thesis (Madison, Wisconsin: Department of Education, University of Wisconsin, 1956).

[12] Ned A. Flanders, *Teacher Influence, Pupils Attitudes and Achievements: Studies in Interaction Analysis*, Cooperative Research Project No. 397 (Minneapolis, Minn.: University of Minnesota, 1960) 121 pp.

[13] Duayne E. Huebner, *From Classroom Action to Educational Outcomes, An Exploration in Educational Theory*, unpublished Ph.D. thesis (Madison, Wisconsin: University of Wisconsin, 1959) 218 pp.

[14] B. Othanel Smith et al., *A Study of Logic of Teaching* (Urbana, Illinois: Bureau of Educational Research, University of Illinois, 1960) 115 pp.

Proctor,[15] and Herrick and Lund,[16] on the analysis of classroom interaction as recorded in teaching-learning episodes, is suggestive of another attack on the problem of curriculum structure. These attempts to explain and account for what happens as a teaching experience unfold with children providing us with first-hand data about the scene where all curriculum planning ultimately resolves itself. It is likely that much new thinking about curriculum development will find its initial stimulus coming from this kind of study.

IN CONCLUSION

It is a thesis of this chapter that no one field of study of discipline is sufficient to be the total basis for adequate curriculum thinking; the anatomy of the teaching-learning task should be a major focus for curriculum plans and for research purporting to have any connection with formal education and its practice. Contributors to curriculum theory must work, therefore, in two ways: from the supporting fields of study to instructional practices and from the instructional task back to the supporting fields. They must be guided at all times by the realization that the ultimate goal to be achieved by such theorizing is improved educational practice.

A second thesis of this paper is that the study of curriculum is fundamentally a study of patterns of interaction and structuring among familiar and well-known components. Uniqueness comes in the patterning, not in the presence or absence of new elements. Simple concepts of causality, linear relationships, and absolute distinctions of goodness and badness are not likely to give much comfort to those involved in curriculum research.

The third premise of this paper is that the task of developing a theory of curriculum and instruction is the distinctive obligation and contribution of professional education to the educational programs of the common schools and colleges of this country. It is here that the contributions of the behavioral and philosophic

---

15 E. Murial Wright and Virginia H. Proctor, *Systematic Observation of Verbal Interaction as a Method of Comparing Mathematics Lessons,* Cooperative Research Project No. 816 (St. Louis, Mo.: Washington University, 1961).

16 Virgil E. Herrick and Grace Lund, *The Curricular Analysis of Teacher-Learning Episodes,* mimeographed paper (Madison, Wisconsin: University of Wisconsin, 1960) 35 pp.

sciences to education find both their justification and focus; the hard fact is that no adequate theory of curriculum and instruction is resolved by the contribution of one academic discipline alone. It is here, also, that studies of administration, finance, school personnel, teacher education, buildings, instructional materials, and the like find the educational referent which gives them point and significance; the equally hard fact is that administration without educational vision, or educational buildings and materials without a source of educational purpose, are important aspects of an educational program without adequate substance or direction.

Many of the suggestions made in this paper grow out of empirical studies which have some research foundations. It is strongly felt, however, that the research methods of curriculum cannot restrict themselves to old classical concepts of the scientific method. We need creative approaches to research methodology as much as we need validation of practice. But as Kelley and Rasey maintain, "New facts call for new doing, and new facts take tenable action out of the realm of opinion. It is necessary to project the meaning of knowledge into practice. . . . The real difficulty is with those who practice in disregard of data and those who have data but do not project them in their meaning for action."[17]

---

[17] Earl C. Kelley and Marie J. Rasey, *Education and the Nature of Men* (New York: Harper & Row, Publishers, (1952) pp. 65–66.

2

Concept of Curriculum Design

*One of the problems facing curriculum theorists
is that of developing useful curriculum designs. What
is the function of a curriculum design in improving
educational programs? What are the important components of a curriculum design? These questions
and several others are answered in this selection,
and eleven propositions concerning curriculum
design are offered.*

D. W. A.
J. B. M.
F. B. M.

Any adequate structure or design of curriculum defines the
important components or aspects of curriculum and determines the
pattern of their relationships to each other and to the curriculum
jobs to be performed. A curriculum pattern provides a consistent
framework of values and their priorities for dealing with the
operational decisions of the teaching-learning situation. A curriculum structure has the quality of a kind of organic unity in which
the dimensions and domains of the educational enterprise are
meaningfully coherent and identifiable.

As one thinks about these statements, it seems that some of
the same ideas are being said again and again. A curriculum
pattern and its attendant theory should be capable of:

1. Accounting for all of the factors that are involved in curriculum.

2. Defining the coherency of these factors both to themselves and to their action points.

3. Predicting and controlling the educational behavior of the learner.

At one level, a curriculum pattern is synonymous with the various approaches commonly talked about in curriculum: the "subject approach," the "broad-fields approach," the "problems-of-living approach," and the "emerging-needs approach" on the elementary school level, and the "subject" and "core-curriculum" approaches at the secondary level. At another level, it has to do with different organizational patterns within a single content field. On still a different level, it exists in a unit of a teaching plan for a single lesson. It is likely that Herbart, Froebel, McMurray, Parker, and Parkhurst, who were concerned with patterns of teaching were dealing with the same problems we are talking about. It is likely that the problems of a single teaching plan, an organizational plan for a subject area, various approaches to the over-all curriculum, and an over-all plan for education in general are merely various dimensions of the same problem of curriculum design. All of the components of a curriculum design are present in some degree at these various levels of planning and organizing.

The expression of these plans in courses of study, handbooks, and teaching programs form some of the source materials and testing grounds for curriculum theory as it relates to organization and structure. These materials evidence, too, the real need to have some understandable framework for giving them meaning and perspective. Curriculum theory must be more than a collection of unrelated individualized bits of bric-a-brac; a curriculum pattern is the only way to give the specifics of curriculum a meaning and a future.

Curriculum design is a statement of the pattern of relationships which exist among the elements of curriculum as they are used to make one consistent set of decisions about the nature of the curriculum of the child. The role of curriculum design in the improvement of educational programs can best be seen in relation to its following functions: (1) as a definer of the elements of curriculum and their pattern of relationships in curriculum development, (2) as a statement of the means used for selecting and organizing learning experiences, and (3) as an indicator of the role of teachers and children in curriculum planning and development.

A DEFINER OF CURRICULUM ELEMENTS AND PATTERNS OF RELATIONSHIP

It is more accurate to say that design does not, in and of itself, define its elements but that design merely presents and makes evident the need for such definition. It is conceivable on one level of definition that different curriculum programs might be concerned with very different specifics. On a more general level of definition, however, it is possible to distinguish the common elements of all curriculum plans.

One way of examining the characteristics common to all curriculum designs is to relate them to the important curriculum decisions teachers must make. It is proposed that any curriculum design must account for, and resolve in some consistent way, the following questions [1] every teacher must ask himself:

1. How can I know the child and prepare and manage a classroom environment which will promote his optimum learning?

2. How can I identify, define, and use my instructional objectives to determine the scope, direction, and emphasis of the child's learning experience?

---

[1] R. W. Tyler has used the following four questions to organize his courses in curriculum: (1) What educational purposes should the school seek to attain? (2) What educational experiences can be provided that are likely to attain these purposes? (3) How can these educational experiences be organized? (4) How can we determine whether these purposes are being attained? The reader will note that Tyler's questions two and three have been incorporated into question three of this paper, as the problems of selection and organization are so closely related that it is frequently more helpful to the teacher to keep the relationship of these dual problems clear. In this paper questions one and four have been added to emphasize the importance of the learning climate and the teaching process in curriculum. These additional questions are considered important because of the conviction that any plan of curriculum improvement is of little value unless it actually influences the instructional practices of teachers. The plan is more likely to influence practices if the problems involved in such practices from the beginning are considered.

3. How can I select and organize these experiences so as to aid the child to achieve worthwhile educational ends?

4. How can I teach or manage the educational process so that these experiences are most effectively utilized by the child to achieve these ends?

5. How can I evaluate so as to determine the extent and quality of the child's development toward these ends?

As one examines these questions, it becomes apparent that, in addition to suggesting the important decisions on curriculum, they imply also the order in which these decisions are made. Persons who have used this implied order as an approach to curriculum improvement have learned, however, that curriculum improvement and the adequate answering of such questions does not proceed in the indicated one-two-three fashion. One soon finds that the learning climate, objectives, and evaluations are merely necessary adjuncts to the main curriculum problem of selecting, organizing, and teaching of the learning experiences. One soon realizes, too, that the products of dealing with one question are carried along and used to deal with every other question, and that this interplay between questions suggests a pattern of factors of curriculum which must operate in some kind of design if teachers are to improve their curriculum decisions. Unfortunately, however, the value of this list of questions is somewhat obscured because of its inability to imply any more than a temporal, serial order of relationships.

Another definition of the elements every curriculum design must include points out that, since every learning situation must include a learner, a purpose, a content, and a process, every curriculum design must also recognize and account for the part these factors play in the learning experiences of children. Further examination of these important aspects of a learning experience will point out that learning does not take place in a vacuum, but that it is essentially social in nature and in context.

This definition of curriculum elements has the value of making clear something which has frequently been misunderstood in curriculum development. This is the fact that every learning experience always involves all four of the above-mentioned elements in some degree. A recognition of this fact, for example, would have eliminated many of the old arguments about the "activity program" on the basis that it was all activity and no purpose and content. All activities have some kind of content and purpose. The curriculum problem is not one of deciding whether it is either-or but one of deciding the combination of these factors which would best produce the effective development of children.

A similar either-or argument was the one about children and content. It was maintained by one side of this argument that, if you considered content at all, you forgot about children. The other side argued that, if you considered children at all, you immediately lost all concern about the content of their experiences. Most people now recognize that the problem of curriculum design is not one of whether you are or are not going to consider either children or content, but is one of knowing that both must be considered. The real problem is to discover how and for what ends.

The problem of either-or positions in curriculum development suggests that the major argument in the development of more adequate curriculum theory is going to be concerned not with the presence or the absence of the factors mentioned above, but with the nature of their pattern of organization and with the order of their priorities in dealing with the major curriculum problem of selecting and organizing learning activities.

This question of definition and determination of relationships can be further illustrated by examining three examples of curriculum design. These designs are those used by the General College staff of the University of Minnesota, by the curriculum consultants of the Thirty School experiment, and by the speaker in the field program of the University of Chicago. The fact that these designs range in focus from the general college to the elementary school makes little difference, as they are all concerned with general education.

Curriculum design of the General College [2]

The staff developing the program of the General College at the University of Minnesota conceived of curriculum development

---

[2] Ivol Spafford, et al., *Building a Curriculum for General Education: A Description of the General College Program* (Minneapolis, Minnesota: University of Minnesota Press, 1943).

as representing a triangle (Fig. 1). The apex of the triangle represents the outcomes sought for students; the base represents the
philosophy of life and education of those responsible for the educational program; one side represents the needs and interests of

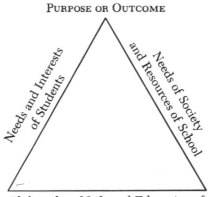

Philosophy of Life and Education of
Those Responsible for Education Programs

FIG. 1.   DESIGN USED BY GENERAL COLLEGE, UNIVERSITY
OF MINNESOTA, IN PLANNING CURRICULUM.

students; the other side, the needs of society and the adequacy of
the resources of the school to meet them.

This design immediately defines for the curriculum worker
what this group considered four important elements in curriculum
development. In addition to the mere listing of the elements to
be considered, the design points out how they are to be combined
to produce a well-balanced curriculum. It suggests further a series
of priorities: (1) that a curriculum is developed on the base of the
educational beliefs and convictions of the persons responsible for
its development; (2) that the purposes of the General College provide the means for selecting and giving direction to the needs of
students; and (3) that the individual needs of students cannot be
considered in isolation but must be recognized in relation to the
needs of society and the capacity of the resources of the school
to meet them.

Unfortunately for the curriculum worker, the stimulation and
suggestion given to his thinking by this diagram is lessened when

he attempts to see how these various elements are different and how they are used to make the decisions important in determining what the curriculum is actually going to be. To be useful to curriculum workers, a curriculum design must have the capacity for helping solve curriculum problems. This design, for example, does not make clear whether the needs of students and society determine the purposes of the General College, or whether the purposes of the General College determine the needs to be met by the instructional program, or whether the needs of students and society serve as both the ends and the means. In each case, the use the staff would make of this design in dealing with the problem of selection would be somewhat different.

Similarly, a philosophy of life and education generally covers such activities as are involved in identifying values, in seeing the consistent relationships which exist between values and human behavior, and in using values to make judgments about the adequacy of means to achieve ends. Would philosophy in this sense be the over-all dynamic process involved in putting a design to work? Or would it be one of its elements in the same way that the needs of students are an element in curriculum design? Is it feasible to use philosophy as a base for curriculum design when it might be more useful if the curriculum worker saw philosophy as a process for putting the whole design to work in making the important decisions on curriculum? Would it be more useful to curriculum development and to the evolving of a more adequate curriculum theory if we were to reveal the precise bases which are actually being used to make these decisions, rather than to cover them up in some vague term like "philosophy?"

> *Proposition 1.* Any curriculum design or plan, if it is to become effective in improving curriculum, must make explicit and clear the bases upon which curriculum decisions are made.

The value of this proposition for curriculum design is clear when one realizes that, unless the bases used for decision-making are recognized, there is little chance for improving the decision or for re-examining the adequacy of the bases.

A major point is made, however, by this statement of the General College in regard to curriculum planning. It points out that curriculum planning must take place in all curriculum development. Actually, there are no unplanned curriculums. It is true that some curriculums are often narrowly conceived and limited, but even the naive question, "What shall we do today?" indicates that some kind of curriculum planning is taking place. Differences of opinion about curriculum planning develop immediately, however, when the "what," "when," and "by whom" aspects of curriculum planning are considered. These differences in how curriculum planning is done are aspects which will distinguish one curriculum design from another.

Curriculum design of the Thirty School experiment [3]

The curriculum consultants of the Thirty School experiment found it exceedingly important that they help the staffs of the schools with whom they worked to see some of the relationships which exist between the important elements of curriculum. They found the diagram in Fig. 2 useful in illustrating the interrelatedness of the four curriculum factors of objectives, methods and organization, subject matter, and evaluation.

Besides showing the interrelatedness of this set of factors in curriculum development, the contribution of this design to staffs working on curriculum is that it suggests the following four helpful questions: What is to be done? What subject matter is to be used? What classroom procedures and school organizations are to be followed? How are the results to be appraised?

For teachers, the value of this design over the diagram used by the General College is that teachers are accustomed to asking these questions and are able to see the relationship of any answers to their own work with children. This design points out these questions and indicates their interrelationships—that is, that objectives serve as a base for determining subject matter and teaching procedures, as well as for evaluation. The design itself lacks any suggestion of means for determining the objectives and the other factors in addition to objectives that should be considered in

---

3 H. H. Giles, S. P. McCutchen, and A. N. Zechiel, "Exploring the Curriculum: The Work of the Thirty Schools from the Viewpoint of the Curriculum Consultants," *Adventures in American Education*, II (New York: Harper & Row, Publishers, 1942) p. 1.

deciding on the subject matter and the instructional procedures of the curriculum.

It is necessary to point out that these two illustrated designs are of different kinds. The General College design was an attempt to describe the components which would have to be considered in making many important curriculum decisions. The objectives, the needs of children, the needs of society, the philosophy of the staff—all are important considerations in the making of curriculum decisions, even though it was shown that the design was incomplete in this respect.

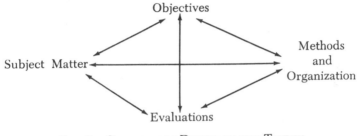

FIG. 2.   CURRICULUM DESIGN OF THE THIRTY
SCHOOL EXPERIMENT.

This design, however, failed to suggest how these components were related to the problems of the teacher and how they were inter-related in dealing with these problems. The Thirty School design is strong at the points where the design of the General College is weak, and weak at the point where the General College design is strong.

This difficulty, as illustrated in the case of these two designs, will be met again and again by the curriculum worker who attempts to use various curriculum designs to make important curriculum decisions. This difficulty is caused by the fact that no one definition of the curriculum components and their interrelationships is suffi-cient in itself. Both the General College design with its statement of some of the elements to be involved in the decisions of cur-riculum, and the Thirty School design with its statement of the factors about which decisions are going to be made are necessary subdesigns within the over-all design of the curriculum. It is quite likely that other definitions of subdesigns are necessary before the curriculum can be seen in its entirety. The design of the curriculum, contrary to most of the thinking about it, is not to be developed in one dimension. The difficulty is in knowing what these dimensions are and how they go together.

> *Proposition 2.* Any over-all curriculum design sufficient to give adequate direction to a program of general education must be considered in more than one dimension and on more than one operational level.

Another curriculum design

The design proposed here (Fig. 3) attempts not only to make more explicit some of the contributions of the General College design but also to continue in the direction of the Thirty School proposal and show how these components actually are focused on the child's curriculum.

The rectangle in the middle of this diagram represents the curriculum of the child. It indicates that t.:s experience should be directed toward the goals of the educational program, that it should have adequate balance, and that it should emphasize or make available learning activities to children when these activities are of greatest importance to the child in his development. As one reads this, he should recognize the number of "value" words in the above sentence—"adequate," "goals," "greatest importance," etc. These value words depend on the other four sides of the rectangle for their definition. The adequacy and the importance of the experiences for the child's development will be determined by the definition and values placed on the elements suggested by the other portions of the diagram.

These learning experiences for children are selected, organized, and developed to achieve the objectives of the educational program, but the objectives provide only one of the bases used in such development. Another base for determining more specifically what experiences should be considered and how they should be organized and developed comes from the understandings held by the staff or teacher concerning the nature of the development of children, how they learn, how one lives democratically, and what should be the function of the school in the education of citizens in a democratic society. The left side of the rectangle indicates the nature of these factors important in the making of curriculum decisions.

Similarly, the nature of the school organization and the instructional resources are a conditioning factor in determining the nature of the experiences children have in school. While it is a truism in educational administration that the organization of the school, along with its resources and facilities, should reflect and implement the educational program, too often such facilities, organization, and administrative procedures have served to prevent and obstruct curriculum improvement. This group of factors, however, does provide the third base for use in providing directives for the curriculum.

The base of the rectangle indicates a problem all teachers must face and one which is not usually recognized in curriculum development. It is the problem of the organization of the learning experiences for children. The previous three bases have been used in the main to select the experiences and to indicate the instructional procedures. These bases fail, however, under most conditions of curriculum development, to indicate to the teacher how he can organize experiences and procedures around some instructional center which enables the learning experiences both to make sense to children and to provide some kind of continuity to the learning. From the point of view of the teacher, the base of the rectangle is the most important part of the design. It indicates the points around which learning experiences can be organized and to which all the other bases make their contribution.

Proposition 3. A curriculum design becomes more usable in improving educational programs if it has as its major organizational focus the problem of selecting, organizing, and teaching the learning experiences of children and youth.

The value of this kind of reference lies in the fact that, in addition to revealing the complex nature of curriculum development and the importance of considering a pattern of factors, it directs attention to the experiences of children and to the centers to use for selecting, organizing, and teaching these experiences in an educational program. This last is a matter considered too infrequently in developing a program at any level. Unless the centers used for organizing learning experiences are considered along with

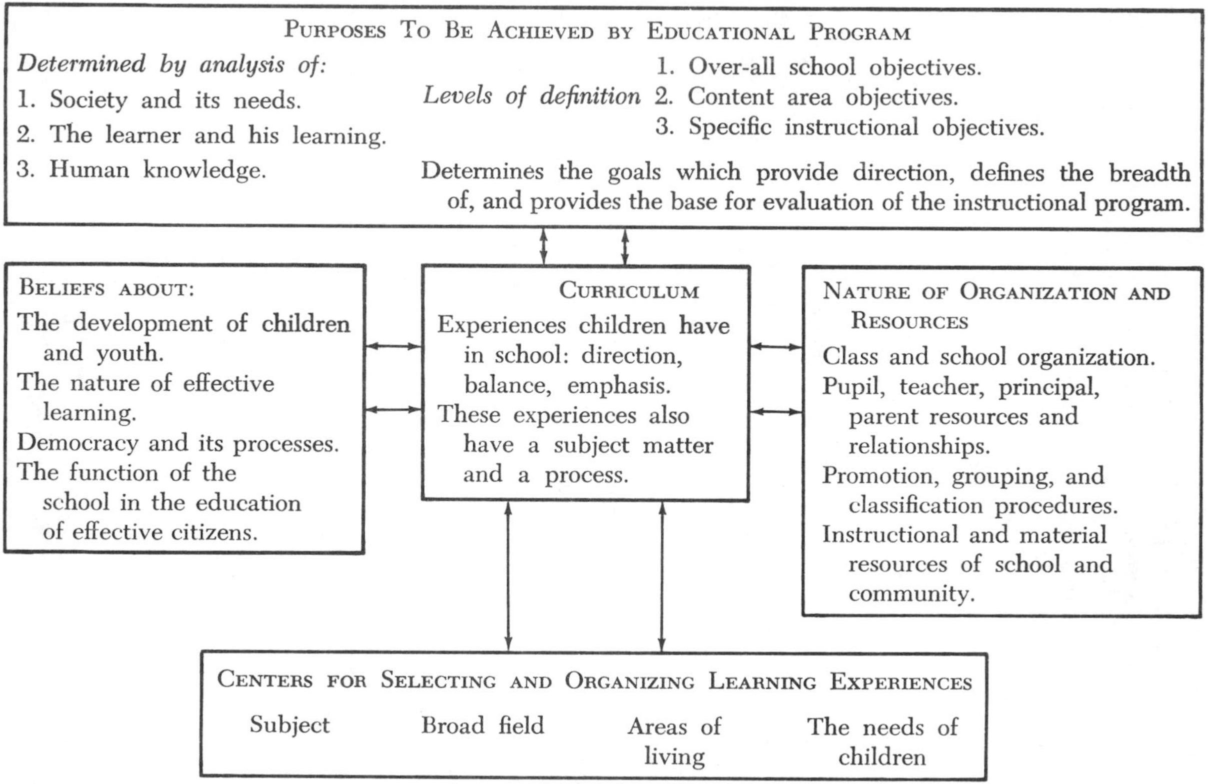

PURPOSES TO BE ACHIEVED BY EDUCATIONAL PROGRAM

Determined by analysis of:

1. Society and its needs.
2. The learner and his learning.
3. Human knowledge.

Levels of definition 1. Over-all school objectives.
2. Content area objectives.
3. Specific instructional objectives.

Determines the goals which provide direction, defines the breadth of, and provides the base for evaluation of the instructional program.

NATURE OF ORGANIZATION AND RESOURCES

Class and school organization.
Pupil, teacher, principal, parent resources and relationships.
Promotion, grouping, and classification procedures.
Instructional and material resources of school and community.

CURRICULUM

Experiences children have in school: direction, balance, emphasis.
These experiences also have a subject matter and a process.

BELIEFS ABOUT:

The development of children and youth.
The nature of effective learning.
Democracy and its processes.
The function of the school in the education of effective citizens.

CENTERS FOR SELECTING AND ORGANIZING LEARNING EXPERIENCES

Subject   Broad field   Areas of living   The needs of children

FIG. 3. A PROPOSED CURRICULUM DESIGN.

28

the definitions of objectives and analyses of behavior which would characterize these objectives, the teacher is left without any means for relating activities, content, and process to objectives in a way which has meaning to children and which would insure some kind of meaningful continuity to the learning program. Anyone who has struggled as a teacher or curriculum worker with objectives operationally defined will recognize the importance of this additional consideration.

Another value found in the use of this design is that it helps the teacher see clearly the bases upon which he selects and organizes teaching activities. The lack of this kind of understanding is one of the reasons why many of the products of curriculum planning and development are not used by teachers in their work with children. The design points out the important distinction between a curriculum analysis where objectives are defined and related learning activities are identified and listed and an instructional organization where such activities take on purpose, relatedness, and perspective. The latter demands an organizing center for including children, for tying up and relating isolated activities, and for providing continuity. This does not mean that curriculum analyses are not important and essential to curriculum development. The thing forgotten, however, is the impossibility of taking a list of analyzed activities and teaching it to children in a way that would be at all meaningful. The next step is to move from the curriculum analyses to a consideration of necessary instructional organizations and developments. This last step insures that what has gone before will make its contribution to the educational program. This step demands, however, that the problem of instructional centers and organization not be attacked as a discrete problem. The concept of curriculum design that is demanded is one in which any attack on the problem of organization is seen as an important phase of a number of equally important considerations.

Incomplete as it is, a final value of this frame of reference is that it suggests a way of resolving a common problem of curriculum development. Should a staff, for example, begin their program of curriculum development with a definition of their purpose, with their beliefs about the development of children, with the content to be taught, or with the nature and organization of resources to be used? This curriculum design suggests, theoretically, that it does not make much difference where a staff begins, as long as the proper factors are considered and the program is carried sufficiently far to insure that all the above approaches will make their contributions to the program being developed. This design points out that no *one* of these common approaches to curriculum development is sufficient unto itself but demands all the rest before a well-conceived educational program can result. The literature of curriculum development is full of descriptions of how the problems of the curriculum were supposedly solved by some particular kind of grouping or school organization, or by the application of some specific teaching technique, or by knowledge of the child.

Proposition 4. A concept of curriculum design is necessary to give perspective and orientation to curriculum-improvement programs concerned with a single phase of curriculum development.

It is the contention of this paper, therefore, that any one of these approaches alone is not sufficient to develop the kind of curriculum necessary to develop well-rounded citizens in a democratic social order. We are gradually accumulating sufficient experience to recognize some of the deficiencies of each of the above common approaches to curriculum development. The resolution of many of these difficulties will be made by moving to a consideration of all that is involved in the proper use of centers for organizing the learning experiences of children and youth.

A STATEMENT OF THE MEANS USED FOR SELECTING AND ORGANIZING LEARNING EXPERIENCES

Any attempt to categorize curriculum approaches on the basis of sharp yes-or-no distinctions about over-all objectives or about the presence or absence of content, process, or learners is doomed to failure. All curriculum designs try to achieve the same over-all objectives and include children, subject matter, and an educational process. Curriculum patterns differ in the way in which these elements are combined and the degree to which each is used to make current decisions, much as a group of architects, using the same basic materials, will create different types of structures.

In examining the problem of design for dealing with the procedures involved in selecting and organizing learning experiences, it is convenient to study design in relation to the four common approaches to the problem of curriculum organization. These approaches are the "subject," the "broad-field," the "problems-of-living," and the "needs" approaches. It is not possible to discuss all and to make comparisons between these approaches in this paper. One—the subject approach—is selected, not because it is illustrative of what the writer considers to be best practice, but because it illustrates *common* practice and thus provides a better vehicle to examine the problem of design than any of the others.

The subject approach

The subject approach to curriculum organization down through history has come to be associated with sharply defined subject divisions, a concern about the understanding of key concepts in each subject field, a way of thinking about these concepts (scientific method in science, historical method in history, etc.), and the stressing of the structure of relationships within which these concepts are organized in order that the learner may remember, understand, and use them.

Means of selection of learning experiences

In the subject organization, the concepts to be learned, with their related intellectual disciplines, form the instructional objectives of content and process for that subject. As such instructional objectives, they provide the first base for identifying all possible experiences, activities, and materials which might be useful in developing and understanding the concepts to be taught and the skills to be mastered. These objectives of content and process are the means through which the over-all objectives of the school are achieved. The subject curriculum says, in effect, that the acquisition of these understandings and intellectual disciplines are the best insurances of a good life and citizenship in a democratic society.

Proposition 5. In curriculum design, the identification of the approach used for selecting and organizing the learning experiences of children determines the nature of the definition and use of objectives at the instructional level.

The concepts, however, are not used by the subject specialist or by the teacher as the final means to select the particular experiences used with a specific group of children. Subsequent screens of selection are the interests and problems of children, the plan of continuity, the ability of children to understand; and the conditions and resources of the teacher, the school, and the community. The order of priority within these screens of selection is concepts and disciplines first, followed by a consideration of what is involved in bringing the interests and understandings of children and the resources of the school to their development. In the needs approach, on the other hand, the need or problem of the group has first priority, and it is used to select the concepts and skills necessary to deal with it adequately. Thus, the factors or steps involved in the selection of learning experiences are not essentially different in the different approaches; they are differentiated primarily on the basis of what is considered most important as an initial base for selection.

Proposition 6. A curriculum design makes clear the factors involved in the selection of learning experiences and indicates the order of priority in which they are used.

Means for organizing learning experiences

The organization of learning experiences can best be discussed in terms of the centers which have been used to organize them. An instructional center is whatever the teacher has used to relate and "tie up" the learning activities of the pupils in some kind of meaningful organization. Common centers have been an interest, a fact or skill to be learned, a job to be accomplished, a problem to be solved, and a question to be answered.

It is not possible to discuss adequately the conditions important in the selection of centers of instructional organization, but any examination at all will point out how necessary it is for subject teachers to move from lists of facts to be learned to the interests, problems, questions, or concerns of the learner or culture as a base for instructional organization.

The major points of this last statement for curriculum design are two.

Propositions 7 and 8. The curriculum design must (a) indicate the nature of the centers used for organizing the instructional program, and (b) point out the extent to which the center of instructional organization becomes not only the focus for organization but also the means for selecting.

This last proposition can best be illustrated by again using a comparison of the "subject" and the "needs" approaches to curriculum planning. In the subject approach the teacher uses the concepts-to-be-learned objectives as a means of selecting the learning experiences. Then he moves on to a consideration of how he can identify some center of interest which he can use as a vehicle to develop an understanding of such concepts. In the needs approach, on the other hand, the need or problem to be attacked serves *both* as selector of the activities and as a center of organization.

One cannot examine the problem of selection and organization very long before realizing that inherent in it is the problem of continuity. In the confines of this paper it is not possible to do more than point out the major importance of the problem of continuity in both selecting and organizing learning experiences. Suffice to say here:

Proposition 9. A curriculum design must make clear the nature and use of the provisions for both horizontal and vertical continuity.

AN INDICATOR OF THE ROLE OF
TEACHERS AND CHILDREN

The role of teachers and children in curriculum development has been a controversial issue in curriculum theory from the time the early cave men tried to set up a "meat-eater" curriculum for individuals with "fish-eating" interests. At the same time, it still is a point of concern to communities, to instructional staffs, to teachers, and to children. Any teacher who is to be at all intelligent about his part in selecting, organizing, and teaching the learning experiences must be able to see clearly his responsibilities in this process and the degrees of freedom he has for carrying them out.

Using the subject approach to curriculum organization again as our example, many teachers are bothered at just this point. They ask: "After I am able to identify and define the concept to be learned, how many degrees of freedom do I have to select the particular experiences and instructional materials; to organize and give direction to the scope, timing, and emphasis of the learning process; and to see the continuities, relationships, and evaluations necessary to determine the next steps?" "What is my role?" "How much responsibility can I assume?" "What is my part in making the major decisions on the curriculum?"

In the subject approach, the teacher usually has very little to do in defining the concepts to be learned, determining their structural organization, or identifying the necessary intellectual disciplines. For most subject teachers, all the above questions are answered for him by the instructional materials. Using a basic textbook and following it closely, the teacher is concerned mainly with the questions and experiences necessary to see whether the child has understood the material presented and with adjusting the timing and evaluations of the learning program to the needs of his pupils. If, however, the teacher is given the responsibilities involved in determining answers to the above questions, he behaves quite differently. The diagram in Fig. 4 presents the problem.

In this diagram, Level III is the subject program where the teacher has the least responsibility for making many of the important decisions regarding the curriculum of the children under his care. Of course, on this level, the role of children is to do or die. As he moves toward Level I, however, the teacher assumes more and more responsibilities for decisions related to the nature of the experiences used, the timing and time schedules, methods of work, and evaluation. One should note, nevertheless, that he still does not determine the concepts to be taught and the continuity of the learning process.

(Read in this direction→)			
Areas of *planning*	*Level* III *determined by*	*Level* II *determined by*	*Level* I *determined by*
Concept to be taught	Text or workbook	Text and course study	Design of curriculum in subject field
Experiences, facts, activities, materials	Text, workbook, and teacher	Text, teacher, group of children	Teacher, group of children, and resources of community in which they live
Timing and time schedules	Text, workbook, teachers, and school program	Teacher and school program	Teacher, group of children, school program
Evaluations	Text, workbook, teacher, school evaluation program	Teacher, concept to be learned, evaluation program	Children, teachers, and school evaluation
Continuities and next steps	Text, workbook, and articulation of school program	Text, course of study, teacher	Design of curriculum, teacher, group of children

FIG. 4. LEVELS OF TEACHER RESPONSIBILITY IN PLANNING
INSTRUCTIONAL PROGRAMS IN THE SUBJECT APPROACH.

After the teacher has decided [4] the level of responsibility within which he wishes to operate, the nature and scope of his activities

---

[4] This decision can be made by the individual teacher, but it is made much easier if he and the whole staff are participants in such decisions and every resource is available to help him make it. Any movement toward Level I demands more skilful teaching, and every teacher needs help in developing such competence.

at this second step in selection is clear. If he is operating at Level III, he is concerned about the interests, questions, and problems of children only incidentally as they can be brought into the discussion of the textbook materials. The teacher is interested primarily in the speed with which children can pass through the material and the degree to which they can understand it. His evaluations are usually in terms of the facts covered by the text and seldom in terms of the concept to be understood, its relationships to other important ideas, and their import for the problems these children face in their living. The next steps of the curriculum are determined by the next page, next chapter, or some such division of the content to be covered.

If, on the other hand, the teacher is operating at Level I, he is immediately plunged into the problems of knowing and working with the children to determine how they can go about understanding the concepts to be learned. He is engrossed in such questions as:

What questions or problems do these children have which may serve as vehicles for developing this concept and showing its relationships to other important concepts?

What kind of learning experiences, materials, and processes are important in dealing with this concept?

How rapidly should we move and to what degree can these children understand this concept at this time?

Are they gaining in competency to think, apply, generalize, and see relationships?

How can we lay the foundations for developing our next concept or a more adequate understanding of the old?

In the needs approach to curriculum organization, the teacher and his group of pupils, with their staff and community resources, must assume the major responsibility for making all essential curriculum decisions. Thus, this point and our examination of the degrees of freedom for the teacher in the subject approach suggest the next proposition for curricular design.

Proposition 10. Curriculum designs must provide staffs and individual teachers with an understanding of their role and responsibilities in making the major decisions of curriculum development.

This proposition points up the value of curriculum design in in-service work with teachers on curriculum. Its value consists primarily of helping teachers see their roles and responsibilities in making the major decisions of curriculum and in aiding them to become more competent in recognizing and using the tools and procedures necessary to make them well. When this is done within the structure of a recognized and understood curriculum approach, the degrees of freedom are much more easily recognized, and the next steps for the teacher and staff to take are much more readily approached.

This last proposition of curriculum design, if recognized adequately, will also eliminate the long-discussed question of planned and unplanned curriculums. The concept of design points out that discussing it is a waste of time. The examination of curriculum approaches and the roles teachers and children play in making the important decisions will keep the attention of workers in curriculum on the "who," "when," "how," and "to-what-degree" aspects of the question. If attention is kept here, it is possible to go back to the basic assumptions regarding the nature of learning and development, the nature of our society and the role of the school in it which underlie and support each approach. The examination of these assumptions provides a more adequate base for reaching conclusions regarding the adequacy of various curriculum approaches than arguments as to whether curriculum is planned or not planned.

Proposition 11. The identification and study of the assumptions underlying the major curriculum approaches provide the means for revealing and pointing up the key research and development problems in curriculum.

CONCLUSION

This paper has made eleven propositions regarding the importance and the function of curriculum design. These propositions are as follows:

1. Any curriculum design or plan, if it is to become effective in improving curriculum, must make explicit and clear the bases upon which curriculum decisions are made.

2. Any over-all curriculum design sufficient to give adequate direction to a program of general education must be considered in more than one dimension and on more than one operational level.

3. A curriculum design becomes more usable in improving educational programs if it has as its major organizational focus the problem of selecting, organizing, and teaching the learning experiences of children and youth.

4. A concept of curriculum design is necessary to give perspective and orientation to curriculum-improvement programs concerned with a single phase of curriculum development.

5. In curriculum design, the identification of the approach used for selecting and organizing the learning experiences of children determines the nature of the definition and use of objectives at the instructional level.

6. A curriculum design makes clear the factors involved in the selection of learning experiences and indicates the order of priority in which they are used.

7-8. The curriculum design must (a) indicate the nature of the centers used for organizing the instructional program and (b) point out the extent to which the center of instructional organization becomes not only the focus of organization but also the means for selecting.

9. A curriculum design must make clear the nature and use of the provisions for both horizontal and vertical continuity.

10. Curriculum designs must provide staffs and individual teachers with an understanding of their roles and responsibilities in making the major decisions of curriculum development.

11. The identification and study of the assumptions underlying the major curriculum approaches provide the means for revealing and pointing up the key research and developmental problems in curriculum.

The teacher and staff having a curriculum design in mind will have a more adequate orientation to the problem of curriculum development, a greater sensitivity to the various possible approaches to their solution, and will be more likely to see how each part of an educational program is related to every other part. This kind of understanding is the best possible assurance for wise and continued development of educational programs for children and youth.

3

A Curriculum Design

What are some of the effects on curriculum-designing operations of using the child, rather than subject matter, as the major referent? What types of planning are necessary for developing an experience curriculum? What are some of the difficulties encountered in developing an experience curriculum?

D. W. A.
J. B. M.
F. B. M.

In the elementary school there are four common patterns of curriculum design: the subject approach, the broad fields approach, the areas or problems-of-living approach, and the needs, or emerging, approach. There are naturally many modifications of these main designs, but their essential ideas hold on both the elementary and the secondary school level. Unfortunately our common-school curriculum theory is somewhat cluttered by the use of different words or phrases for the same idea—principally because the curriculum workers at either level know little about what the workers at the other level are doing and, as a consequence, are constantly coining new phrases for old ideas.

To give clarity to the discussion, one should sketch the contrasting ideas in each approach in order that the problem of

39

planning in a specific design can be seen in bold relief. Because of space limitations, this procedure is obviously impossible. Suffice it to say, however, that these four designs profess to achieve the same general over-all objectives; all involve also a content, a process, and children. They distinguish themselves from one another primarily in the priority of the different bases used for selecting and organizing the learning experiences and in the role of the children and teacher in the planning of their curriculum.

THE EXPERIENCE CURRICULUM

As has been stated previously, there is, in reality, no "unplanned curriculum," although the term is at times applied to the approach variously called the *needs, experience,* or *emerging curriculum,* in which less emphasis is placed on planning in advance the specific problems to be solved, the content to be learned, and the skills to be mastered. In the experience-curriculum approach, more emphasis is placed on teacher-pupil planning and on how a teaching staff and their educational community can accomplish the educational planning essential to giving adequate meaning, scope, and direction to the learning experiences of the children intrusted to their care.

In speaking of the experience curriculum, Hopkins quoted the following definition from the "Syllabus for Educational Foundations, Section I, Semester, 1936:" [a] series of purposeful experiences growing out of pupil interests and moving toward an ever more adequate understanding of, and intelligent participation in, the surrounding culture and group life." [1] The experience curriculum, then, has its beginning in the situations which confront children in their immediate living. The concerns of children in meeting these situations form the bases upon which the curriculum of any particular child and his group will be built. Whether these concerns are called "interests," "needs," "purposes," "problems," "upsets," or any other name makes little difference so long as the

---

[1] L. Thomas Hopkins, *Integration: Its Meaning and Application* (New York: Appleton-Century-Crofts, 1937) p. 253.

learning situation meets certain conditions: (1) It must revolve about problems which are germane to youth; (2) it must be concerned with vital and crucial aspects of the world in which youth is learning to live; and (3) it must call for dynamic and creative behavior on the part of the learner. A sound integrated curriculum would thus consist of a succession of natural and vital units of experience, each centering about a real problem, each drawing upon subject matter as needed, irrespective of boundary lines, and each eventuating in growth in capacity to live.[2]

The experience curriculum emphasizes the immediate conditions surrounding the child and his concerns or purposes as the central basis for educational planning. It suggests that the teacher and his group of children are the major planning unit. All other resources for this planning are seen as elements which enter this process only as they become necessary to the group in order to deal with its problem adequately and to gain a more adequate understanding of, and intelligent participation in, the surrounding culture and group life. Such planning by the teacher and the group is a continuous examination and study of the group's ongoing experience made for the purpose of discovering the nature of the next step, the appropriate subject matter, ways of attacking the problem, the necessary learning materials and activities, and important abilities and social processes. Such specific items cannot be anticipated in advance, and, therefore, all planning of this nature which is done by agencies other than the learners themselves imposes restriction without knowledge of the situation.

Planning under these conditions is planning as an integral part of the learning process and does not permit any schematic arrangement of things to be accomplished or the development of a curriculum framework which is agreed upon by the school staff in advance and which would develop the scope and sequence of the learning program from the kindergarten through grade twelve. In this design the scope of the curriculum consists in the scope of the child's world at the moment—a scope which will broaden

---

[2] William A. Smith, "Integration: Potentially the Most Significant Forward Step in the History of American Secondary Education," *California Journal of Secondary Education*, X (April, 1935) p. 270.

and deepen as rapidly as his world can be extended, and no more rapidly. The sequence of the curriculum is determined by the conscious continuity of the child's learning experience.

The personal concerns of the child and the development of his concerns provide the basis for dealing with the social needs of the society in which he lives. His life within his group is the basis upon which he extends his knowledge and grasp of all group life. The idea is commonly expressed by the phrase, "If you take care of the present, the future will take care of itself."

Planning by the teacher

The individual teacher and his group are the focus for all planning in the experience curriculum. The teacher is the only person who has access to the raw data with which to make the necessary judgments related to the six major questions of curriculum that he and his children must face and answer. In his planning, the basis for making these decisions is always the child. Thus, the teacher in his planning is constantly coming back to the following question:

How can I know these children so that we can do the teacher-pupil planning necessary to:

1. Develop the kind of social and emotional climate which will leave these children free to express their concerns and use their intelligence in dealing with their problems? (The teacher asks himself, "Can I accept these children both emotionally and intellectually?")

2. Identify and define the major concerns growing out of the situations that confront these children?

3. See the different ways in which these concerns can be attacked, identify the personal and material resources which are necessary, and provide the ideas and facts (subject matter) for dealing with these concerns adequately at this time?

4. Determine the nature of the testing and selection processes which are appropriate and select and use those ideas and skills which are pertinent to the problem being attacked?

5. Help these children to evaluate the extent to which they are achieving their purposes and are developing competency to deal with their problems on increasingly mature levels?

6. Plan with other persons who are important in helping these children relate their own concerns to the surrounding culture and group life?

7. Examine constantly the problem which is being attacked, the activities which are being carried on, the abilities and skills which are being developed, and the understandings which are being gained, in order to see the next steps and the breadth and depth of the experience necessary to these children at this time?

8. Develop the individual and group records which will be helpful in determining the nature of the learning program over a period of time?

Any casual examination of these questions will certainly indicate the nature and quality of the teacher-pupil planning going on in what has often been called the "unplanned curriculum."

Planning by the staff

As has been said, the basic planning unit of the experience curriculum is the teacher and the class group. This group, however, must be related not only to the larger group of the school but also to its own continuous development over the period of the common school. This horizontal and vertical development, which transcends the individual group and the one or more years of experience with one teacher, demands continuous staff planning. Planning at the staff level to insure continuous, broadly conceived development at the pupil-teacher level involves a number of important considerations. These considerations are as follows:

1. Since no one teacher is all things to a child for all time, we, as a staff, must recognize and understand the common values of the educational program. Our planning is concerned with seeing the importance of these values for our instructional practices.

2. Since we are unable to determine the content of the child's experience in advance, we as a staff need to perfect our understanding of the child and the nature of the educational process which will aid in his educational development. Our planning is concerned with our understanding and our ability to practice this educational process ourselves in working on our staff problems and in working with children.

3. Since we are dealing with children in constant interaction with their culture, we, as a staff, must be in touch with this culture and study it in order to understand better its influence and part in the development of children. Our planning is related to being aware of the school's role in our particular community, the part it should play, and the nature of our educational contribution.

4. Since the teacher-pupil class group lives in a larger school group, we, as a staff, must see how we can manage the total school environment and resources in order to make sure that time, facilities, and resources are making their contribution to educational development. Our planning is concerned with time arrangements, co-operative use of facilities, co-operative use of the instructional materials, and the nature of records and reports. This planning may be between two teachers, or it may encompass the whole staff.

5. Since the leadership role is one of responsibility to people, to values and ideas, and to an educational process, this responsibility must be seen in relation to implementing the personal-social concerns of children which form the matrix for curriculum organization.

Planning at the community level

The teacher-pupil group, the staff, and the community do not exist as separate, self-sustaining planning groups. As teacher-pupil planning is reinforced and extended by staff planning, so school planning is reinforced and extended by community planning. The persistent personal problems of the children are merely extensions of the persistent personal social problems of the community in which they live.

The basic idea underlying the experience curriculum is that it is an integral part of the same social process carried on by the community of which the school is a part. One important concern of a community is the difficulty involved in identifying and defining its common problems. The community is constantly involved in trying to discover better ways to solve these problems, in making up its corporate mind regarding the procedures to use, in selecting and using its personnel and material resources, in evaluating its accomplishments to date, and in seeing its next steps. The community, therefore, is constantly engaged in the same kind of problems, utilizing many of the same processes, and illustrating all the problems of planning, as the teacher, pupil, and staff of its school are illustrating in their own practices. Thus, planning on any one of these levels must not only be related to planning at each separate level but must also be seen as parallel interrelated enterprises at each level. The leadership of the school is involved at each level, and the school should assume some responsibility for making sure that the lines of communication are kept open between planning groups and that adequate planning is being done at the proper time and at the proper level.

Planning, in view of these considerations, consists not in setting up routines of things to do in one-two-three order, but in planning in light of the factors which are in constant interaction with one another.

BASIC CONCEPTS UNDERLYING THE EXPERIENCE CURRICULUM

The experience curriculum cannot be properly understood unless one realizes that this curriculum is based on a concept of what the educational requirements of a democratic society are. This concept stresses the analysis of ongoing experience in order to identify the problems which grow out of that experience and which demand some kind of problem-solving activity on the part of the learner. This process is one of the responsibilities of the citizen living in a democratic society—a responsibility which he cannot meet at the adult level without a long-time opportunity to meet problems at every point in his development.

The most important resources that the citizen brings to this problem are his intelligence and his ability to use his past experience and whatever learning resources are available to deal with the problem as intelligently as possible. Planning is involved in this process as an essential element. It is reasoned that, if these are the abilities of a citizen in a democracy, then opportunities for their practice and development should be an important part of any educational program in that society.

Other important ideas in this curriculum design are related to experience, learning, culture, understanding society, and continuity. Although these ideas are important, they cannot be developed here, because major emphasis is being placed on the problem of planning.

PROBLEMS OF PLANNING IN THE EXPERIENCE CURRICULUM

As one studies the responsibilities of the individual teacher, the school staff, and the community for planning, many of the problems confronting this curriculum design are revealed. Some of them are as follows:

1. Teachers and teaching staffs have had little experience in this kind of planning in their own training and in their work as teachers. At the same time, planning of this nature is a highly skilled and complicated process. Any school system developing this curriculum design should realize the need for development of the teacher and staff, for it demands the highest type of leadership.

2. Teachers and teaching staffs are not accustomed to making the decisions involved in this approach. They need to have training and opportunity for practice in using the curriculum tools of selection and organization of learning experiences. The community and the teaching staffs do not move to this design in one full swoop. Attaining this design demands that we practice what we teach—a great strain on any educational program.

3. Elementary schools, in general, have few instructional materials available. The experience curriculum not only demands many instructional materials but requires that they be used in relation to an educational program developing out of the experience of children.

4. Few elementary-school teachers have the broad cultural training necessary to assure that the child has access to man's ideas and ways of thinking about the problem which the child faces. A program of this type demands, in particular, that the teacher be skilled in dealing with problems, in co-operative action, in using instructional resources, and in the arts of language and expression. The teacher's educational values and concepts of learning have to be more than mere words.

5. The development of an experience curriculum must grow out of the thinking and planning of the community itself. Unfortunately, life in America is discrete, and our culture is not well integrated. Often schools are not located in well-integrated communities where the planning just described can take place. Many of our urban districts are the best illustrations of this fact.

Several of these problems are not unique to the experience curriculum but confront every attempt to improve the educational program in our schools.

SUMMARY STATEMENT

The experience curriculum is planned by the children, the teacher, the teaching staff, and the community. Curriculum planning, from the point of view of this conception, is not something which is done before the learning takes place, but is an essential part of the learning process itself and must be carried on so long as learning or life persists. Thus curriculum planning is seen as a fundamental part of the development of a person living and learning in a democratic society.

4

Directives For Curriculum Planning

What is the overarching purpose of education? The relationship between this question and three curricular approaches is demonstrated in this selection. The three approaches are compared in terms of their implications for the role of the teacher, ideas about learning, ideas about the nature of the learner, and other value commitments. How each of the three approaches can be used for specific purposes is indicated. The concept of structure is given fresh meaning as a "necessary aspect of all experience" and is shown to be a major referent for curriculum design. The selection concludes with several generalizations relating to the dilemmas of the curriculum planner.

D. W. A.
J. B. M.
F. B. M.

THE OVERARCHING PURPOSE OF EDUCATION

The different approaches to curricular planning are, in a sense, merely different educational plans based on different rationales for achieving a much more common agreement about what constitutes the ultimate goal of education. To common earlier

48

statements that the basic purpose of education is to create an "educated" man, "to pass on the cultural heritage," or "to develop the good citizen in a democracy," the following have been added more recently:

The specific task of education must be identified within the context of the primary function of education, which is the achievement and dissemination of knowledge, the cultivation of the intellect, and induction into the uses of reason. Only when the schools energies are centered on these intellectual purposes will it also contribute effectively to the artistic, moral, and spiritual life of the individual and society.

> Sterling M. McMurrin, U.S. Commissioner of Education. Address delivered before the first general session of the Conference on the Ideals of American Freedom and the International Dimensions of Education (Washington, D. C., March 26, 1962).

[These are] the great basic goals of our educational system: to foster individual fulfillment and to nurture the free rational and responsible men and women without whom our kind of society cannot endure. Our schools must prepare *all* young people, whatever their talents, for the serious business of being free men and women.

> John W. Gardner in *Goals for Americans, The Report of the President's Commission on National Goals.* The American Assembly, Columbia University Spectrum Book (Englewood Cliffs, N.J.: Prentice-Hall, Inc., 1960) p. 100.

The central aim of education, then, is to develop rational men who do not sin against themselves and their kind. The rational man not only is committed to the rich fruits of injury but also is prepared to act and, indeed, acts upon insight rendered compelling by commitment. He knows, as perhaps the most vital ingredient of his rationality, that only through action following understanding and commitment does man forge the links in the chains of his own humanity and of mankind's immortality.

> John I. Goodlad, *Some Propositions in Search of Schools* (Department of Elementary School Principals, N.E.A., 1201 Sixteenth Street, N.W., Washington 6, D. C., 1962) pp. 8–9.

There are still other goals, of course, and each can be stated in somewhat different words. . . . But all tend to fuse together toward one overarching goal. This might be called "social-self-realization," a term which symbolizes the desire of most men for the richest possible fulfillment of men through groups and institutions.

> Theodore Brameld, *Education for the Emerging Age* (New York: Harper & Row, Publishers, 1961) p. 93.

We may take as perhaps the most general objective of education that it cultivate excellence; but it should be clear in what sense this phrase is used. It here refers not only to schooling the better student but also in helping each student achieve his optimum intellectual development. . . . One thing seems clear: if all students are helped to the full utilization of their intellectual powers, we will have a better chance of surviving as a democracy in an age of enormous technological and social complexity.

> Jerome S. Bruner, *The Process of Education* (Cambridge, Mass.: Harvard University Press, 1962) pp. 9–10.

While the desire and the ability to learn are not shared equally by everyone, both can be fostered by good teaching, by careful guidance, by building and enlarging sympathetic enclaves, and by providing a range of educational opportunities. These tasks are too great for partial and divided efforts. The inquiring minds of the past have produced most of the advances of civilization. Our hopes for the future must rest in a large measure on our capacity to increase the number and ability of those who continue all their lives to share in the benefits and pleasures of intellectual inquiry.

> Cyril O. Houle, *The Inquiring Mind* (Madison, Wisconsin: The University of Wisconsin Press, 1961) p. 82.

The primary aim of education in the broadest sense of the word is . . . to help a child of man to attain his full formation or his completeness as a man.

> Jacques Maritain, "Thomist Views on Education" in *Modern Philosophies and Education,* Fifty-fourth Yearbook of the National Society of Education, Part I (Chicago: University of Chicago Press, 1955) p. 62.

I believe it will have become evident why, for me, adjectives such as happy, contented, enjoyable, do not seem quite appropriate to any general description of this process I have called psychological health, even though the person in this process would experience each one of these feelings at appropriate times, but the adjectives such as enriching, exciting, rewarding, challenging, meaningful seem much more appropriate. This process of healthy living is not, I am convinced, a life for the fainthearted. It involves stretching and growing, of becoming more and more of one's potentialities. It involves the courage to be. It means launching oneself fully into the stream of life. Yet the deeply exciting thing about human beings is that when the individual is inwardly free, he chooses this process of becoming.

> Carl R. Rogers, "Toward Becoming a Fully Functioning Person" in *Perceiving, Behaving, Becoming: A New Focus,* Arthur W. Combes, ed. ASCD Yearbook, N.E.A. (Washington 6, D.C., 1962) p. 32.

These excerpts from the writings of a wide range of individuals vitally and thoughtfully concerned with the essential purpose of American education are different in their various degrees of confidence that knowledge, intelligence, and reason *per se* will lead to appropriate value commitments and effective personal and social action. These men are alike, however, in their concern for the individual—that his education will lead him to his fullest realization as a person and as a member of humanity. The "social-self-realization" of Brameld, "becoming a fully functioning person" of Rogers, and "his full formation and completeness as man" of Maritain expresses this well. The tone of these statements is optimistic; their faith is that the development of man's intelligence and rational powers will lead to understanding and that he must become a more responsible and active agent for his own learning and development. Key words are "self-realization," "reason," "understanding," "commitment," "action," and "excellence."

The point of these excerpts is that their focus is on people, on their fullest development, and on the qualities and processes which will make such development possible both now and in the future. The emphasis is not on the nature of the subject matter which will assist and support this development; neither is it on persistent life situations, broad fields in inquiry, or common developmental tasks. These latter considerations are merely possible curricular strategies for developing the kind of person envisioned by these overarching concepts of the central purpose of education.

If we are not to take these conceptions of the central purpose of education lightly, our educational planning, as it attempts to achieve these ends, must envision the central role of the learner in such programs; must provide the maximum development of all individuals and not just a selected few; must develop the skills and attitudes which promote rational behavior; and, finally, must present the conditions which enable a student constantly to grow in the confidence and maturity of his own selfhood in the complex and demanding society and world in which he lives.

THE NECESSARY REFERENTS FOR CURRICULUM PLANNING

Three common referents are used to make the many critical decisions found in the development of any educational program designed to achieve particular ends. These are man's organized knowledge, the society in which he lives, and himself as a learning, developing organism.

These three referents have given rise to the three basic curricular patterns. These are different from each other primarily by the extent to which subject matter and its various categories, or the society and its persistent problems of living and related social processes, or the individual and his perceived concerns and emergent experiences are used as the initial and overriding referents for planning a curriculum. In each approach or design, however, the other referents are considered and used in appropriate ways. The argument, then, is not subject matter versus social orientation versus concern for people and their capacities and development tasks, but it is, rather, a question of which referent offers the most useful over-all structure within which the others can be most effectively included to provide a learning program of adequate quality and breadth.

It is foolish to argue, therefore, that any adequately conceived curriclum based on subject matter does not consider the social consequence of such subject matter, or that the individual and his capacities and interests for learning are not related to the planning. It is just as foolish to believe that any curriculum planning based on a societal conceptual frame or on a concept of the emergent development of the individual does not appreciate and respect subject matter. In fact, more subject matter rather than less is examined and selected because of its relevancy to the problems being attacked, or to the personal concerns being solved. It is true, however, that the structure of the social setting being developed or the perceived structure of the child's phenomenological field is the referent used for planning, rather than the structure of the subject matter being studied. The curricular choice, then, is centered in the nature of the basic orientation and in the resultant structure of curricular operations derived from this orientation. It eliminates the single arbitrary choice of subject matter, of society, or of the individual.

CURRICULUM APPROACHES AND RELATED VALUE ORIENTATIONS

Each of these characteristic approaches to curriculum planning is substantiated by its own philosophic concept of knowledge, man, and value, and with its corresponding concept of learning and development. The common discovery is that there is not one, but many, possible philosophic or psychological positions on any of the important problems of instruction and curriculum development; each supports a particular way of regarding man, his nature, and his education.

Perhaps this is why many of us who work with teachers and programs of in-service education tend to agree with Prescott, who says that no lasting and significant change will take place in a teacher's instructional practices and in the way she will regard and treat children until a corresponding change takes place in her valuing and feeling pattern to support and direct such changes. It should be clear that, with the subject structure, there is more authority in terms of knowing the important concepts and processes to be learned, the relationships to be seen, and the applications to be made. The roles of the teacher and the student vary according to the degree to which these become absolute and the extent to which the student is seen merely as an organism to be surrounded with appropriate clues, feedback mechanisms, and programmed instructional materials.[1] These practices are supported by concepts of what knowledge is of greatest worth, by generalizations as to the nature of intelligence, by doctrines of readiness and interest, by principles of concept formation, and by a faith in primary and secondary reinforcement theory or learning.

---

[1] Burrhus F. Skinner, *Walden II* (New York: The Macmillan Company, 1948) 266 pp.

On the other hand, if the curriculum structure uses persistent problems of living and social processes or the emergent perceptual world of the child as a referent framework for instructional planning and practice, the teacher tends to see the learner as a person with goal perceptions of his own. She sees him with the capacity to identify and select his important learning goals, with ability to test and verify his methods of inquiry, and with the capacity to decide the nature of and uses to be made of emergent generalizations and procedures of decision-making. Intelligence is seen as a dynamic developing capacity influenced by the background and experience of the learner; emphasis is placed on creativity, heuristic thinking, and insight. The picture of the learning process is goal-centered, phenomenological, or topological. The important organizing center is the learner himself.

IMPLICATIONS OF OUR BELIEFS
ABOUT PROCESSES

These distinctions naturally are not absolutely definitive and in reality consist of directions in thinking and the conceptions of man, education, and the learning process. Our proposition is that if we believe that we are helping to develop free, responsible, and creative men who use their rational processes to give direction to their personal and social living, then our educational planning and instructional practices must provide an opportunity for the practice of free, responsible, creative learning. Decisions and judgments as to the significance of this learning based on rational processes and tested by consequences in the quality of present and future use will result.

If we believe in the importance of goal direction and in the value of a purposeful self-evaluating individual then our curriculum thinking and the structuring of our teaching practices cannot deny and prevent such development.

If we believe in the critical importance of a structure and in the process of inquiry and rational thinking, then our students must have opportunities to use, test, and create for themselves, ways to better organize and relate the important meanings their study has for their area of inquiry, for themselves as persons, and for all humanity.

Processes of thinking, communication, human relations, and effective use of resources do not have much meaning in the words we use to talk about them; their meaning comes only as they are used to deal with significant problems and as they make some critical difference in the learning and living experiences of the student. The teacher should see these processes as having important places in the development of the learning experiences of every child at every level of his educational program. If important concepts can provide useful themes throughout programs of general education, how much more critical would it be to see important processes as the essential conveyors for learning at every level of a student's educational existence.

CONTRIBUTIONS OF EACH
CURRICULAR APPROACH

From the foregoing it should be clear that the emphases of the curriculum patterns based on social and individual centers can make contributions of various kinds to our present curriculum with its firmly entrenched subject structure. This will be discussed later, but curriculum patterns based on social orientations are directly relevant to the area of social studies and the social aspects of the school. Concepts of the emergent curriculums are also valuable in expanding the responsible and constructive role of the learner in the learning and evaluation processes, in determining the climate of the learning enterprise, in accepting and respecting the student, and in the critical place that important intellectual and social processes have in the behavior of the classroom.

These curriculum patterns, too, when evaluated from the point of view of use outside of the formal school and from the kind of "curriculum pattern" life itself will offer in the years after school, will indicate the increasing value of concepts based on the social framework and emergent curriculum thinking. The serious consideration of an emergent curriculum structure for planning the in-service program of our schools, and for developing educational programs in communities and less privileged nations is urged.

It has long been noted that a teacher with a fixed subject framework is a poor teacher in programs of special education, in adult education, and in developing programs with people in under-privileged areas. These considerations clearly suggest the need for greater insight by teachers and college professors in the variety of ways in which common goals of education can be effectively realized.

FACING THE IMPLICATIONS OF OUR SUBJECT-ORIENTED SCHOOLS

One of the hard facts of curriculum planning is that the pre-vailing basis for curriculum design is subject matter. The subject matter areas determine the range of educational enterprises which occupy the attention of students and teachers and which deter-mine units for planning staff, time, and building utilization. This is the structure in which most students are educated and most teachers trained, and it forms the context for most of the efforts to improve the quality of our educational programs at the present time.

Rather than to deplore this fact, it seems that the constructive position would be to identify a number of concerns which ought to be considered in our efforts to improve education planning and development.

1. Our overarching goals for education are stated in terms of free men—their qualities of rational behavior and their com-mitments and responsibilities for effective personal and social action. Yet the educational programs designed to achieve these ends are rooted in subject-matter compartments and in the dis-tinctive structures and disciplines of these areas, which are deter-mined quite apart from men and the social context in which they live. Does this gap between our essentially personal and social goals and our essentially subject-oriented instructional pattern cause our goals to be conceived as fine verbalisms to be placed on mastheads and forgotten? Other than to claim that each particular subject area is the most important vehicle for its accomplishment, frequently no one has any intention of using these statements to make any difference.

2. Three notions are considered to be important aspects of a subject: (a) that it has a body of substantive material which can be identified and distinguished from other bodies of content; (b) that this body of content can be arranged and related in a structure which gives these particulars meaning and forms the basis for their retention and transfer to specifics which are relevant to the field considered; and (c) that this subject has a distinctive intellectual discipline through which the substance of the field has been discovered and verified and by which its structure of key relationships is applied to new situations. It is frequently assumed by those working in these fields that their own particular field is of primary significance in achieving our overarching goals of education, and that it is possible to determine a hierarchy of importance among content areas.

If these are the necessary conditions and claims of a subject area, it is possible to raise grave questions as to whether or not such common areas as the language arts, the practical and fine arts, health and physical education, etc. are really subjects because of their lack of a recognizable body of content, a logical structure, and an intellectual discipline. Mathematics is different from science and social studies in that its concepts are abstractions without a necessary referent to particular objects and situations. History, also, if it is considered to be more than a discipline, is forced to gain its content from the subject matter whose history it examines. Thus, we have a history of science, of New York, of ideas, of people, and of things.

If the above is true, then a number of points seem to follow:

1. Will not any attempt to limit our conception of an adequate educational program to the "hard," or basic, subjects prevent an adequate consideration of other necessary areas such as the arts, health, and physical education in our planning? Yet, can any adequate program of general education exist without them?

2. Do not the different natures of subject areas now included in our curriculum demand that different kinds of instructional structures be examined as to their appropriateness for each area? A real opportunity for creative and imaginative curriculum planning confronts those individuals working in all areas. It is particularly important that the nature of the language arts and other

arts be recognized and that their contributions be utilized in appropriate planning rather than to borrow arbitrarily from another area different in its essential nature.

3. Efforts to subdivide and particularize subject fields should not prevent the continuation of the long-time effort of trying to find a common framework within which the divisions of science, mathematics, social studies, and the arts of language could be encompassed. A program of general education should include as few organizing units as possible, so that time and resources are available for breadth and depth of understanding and contribution.

4. Important contributions are to be made in subject development, therefore, at the three points of determining the important content of each field, the particular structures which give them meaning, and the nature and use of the important methods of inquiry in each field. Because these contributions fit into most teachers' curricular framework, they will be seen as important and directly relevant to the teaching each is now doing. Consequently, the willingness to use these contributions, is much greater than if this were not true.

This is the area in which the scholars of each discipline can contribute most. One of the most important recent contributions to curriculum planning has been the contribution of the committees and groups working in mathematics, physics, biology, language, and more recently in English, economics, anthropology, and social studies. The updating of instructional materials, the exploration of various teaching strategies, the use of a wide variety of instructional aids, and the development of related programs of teacher education are having a significant effect on instruction in these areas.

This effort, notwithstanding its importance, has its price tags. The elementary and high school programs are becoming battlegrounds of competing subject-area groups; grim battles are raging for priority in time, in staff, in facilities, and in requirements. Where does one find an over-all conception of the curriculum which will help make such decisions on more than a power or prestige basis? Some of the claims and counterclaims as to the virtue and need for each particular subject area add little to each group's basic integrity and the critical use of its intellectual faculties.

A great gain has been made in updating curriculum content. Some researchers have advocated commissions to accomplish this task every ten to twenty years. The important question is, however, can we wait for such commissions? It is vital that there be ways for improving continuously the content of each subject area. The real safeguards for up-to-date ideas lie in the continuous use of resources, in the teaching of each area in such fashion that the very best in instruction and library resources are used, and in the planning of the instructional program on a basis more comprehensive than the content and pattern of a single textbook.

5. A final concern growing out of the almost exclusive dependence on one curricular pattern is that the study and creative development of alternative ways for structuring and organizing instructional programs may be greatly restricted. The period of the late twenties through the Depression was a time of great invention and experimentation in ways to plan and develop significant programs of instruction on both elementary and college levels. The secondary school was influenced less by such innovations. At present, little creative work is being done in the area of curricular design. It is likely, however, that the present intense interest and concern for education and its learning processes cannot help but provide the thrust for a new period of development in this field.

STRUCTURE AND ITS MEANING

One of the significant emphases in present-day curriculum planning is the concern for going beyond learning of factual information and major generalizations to the structure of relationships which generate a context of meaning and application.

One of the problems, however, has been the confusion and lack of appreciation of structure as a necessary aspect of all experience. The question is not one of structure versus no structure; it is, rather, one of *which* structure and to what degree of inclusion and abstraction it should be developed in order that it become a helpful framework for dealing with a given field of endeavor.

Jerome Bruner, in *The Process of Education*,[2] has summarized most of the salient arguments for structure: (1) that if one understands fundamental ideas of a subject, the subject becomes more comprehensible in the sense that many specifics are illuminated and placed in context; (2) that if details are placed in a structured pattern, they are remembered better; (3) that if fundamental ideas and principles are grasped, the basis and assurance for transfer of this knowledge to other areas and points of application are provided; and (4) that if the structure of a field is grasped, the gap between advanced knowledge and "elementary" knowledge is narrowed.

One can only agree with Bruner and many others who have advanced the arguments that structure is vital in efficient learning and that there is growing evidence that many of these claims are soundly based. No one who is familiar with the full range of instruction in elementary, secondary, and collegiate institutions would do anything but applaud any concept which would force instruction to go beyond specifics, emphasis on memory, and mere accumulations of information.

What is frequently ignored is that this notion of structure and its properties is not restricted to subject fields and that it is found in any area of inquiry in many forms and on many levels of completeness.

Schwab, in his excellent paper, "Education and the Structure of the Disciplines,"[3] points out that investigators in any area of study ask different questions of their field, conceive of its essential nature in different ways, and consequently to different kinds of research, offer different kinds of explanation, and create different theoretical frameworks. He borrows from Auguste Conte's hierarchy of "positive sciences," which runs as follows:

Social sciences
Psychology

---

[2] Jerome Bruner, *The Process of Education* (New York: Harper & Row, Publishers, 1960).

[3] Joseph Schwab, "Education and the Structure of the Disciplines," paper prepared for the Project on the Instructional Program of the Public Schools, N.E.A. (Washington 6, D.C.) pp. 16–18. Found also in July, 1962, issue of the *Educational Record*, published by the American Council of Education (Washington, D.C.) pp. 197–205.

Biology
Chemistry
Physics
Mathematics

Roughly speaking, the variety and number of structures in each discipline is greater as one moves up the list. Physics has only a few, two or three; biology, five or six; social sciences, many.

In general, the greater time man has to study a field and accumulate knowledge about it, the fewer basic structures are used to deal with the knowledge of the fields. A second important point to consider is that a structure dealing with the same particulars may be logical, operational, sequential, and topological in character. The same set of particulars frequently can be organized according to a number of different structures as different questions are asked and as different purposes are achieved.

A third point, substantiated by recent research in perceptual learning, suggests that an important part of learning, besides applying a known structure, is the act of creating and developing a structure within which the particulars can be arranged and handled. Evidence of this phenomena may be found in our own studies (at the University of Wisconsin) which show that the reader's perceptions regarding the nature and structure of reading materials affects the pattern of reading skills and reading rate. This suggests that we must move from preconceived structures to the process of structuring the learning act if we are fully to release and use the intellectual and creative powers of our students. It is clear that instructional patterns which are organized around problem areas, major questions, and concern with persistently recurring issues are more likely to afford an opportunity for the student to become a skilled and active agent in organizing and relating his knowledge in more useful ways and to deal with its conditions and nature appropriately. This use of structuring—rather than *a structure*—as an important part of learning can be applied to all areas and to all curricular patterns. It is perhaps the most exciting directive the present studies and emphases on structure have made. Actually, as one moves from subject matter to socially or individually patterned programs, more rather than less emphasis is placed on the critical importance of the process of structuring as a necessary part of learning.

A fourth point is that program planners in teacher education need to develop a framework which is sufficiently comprehensive to include the dimensions of the teaching act, programs of general education, and knowledge of the foundational fields of learning, human development, and philosophic considerations. This represents the professional knowledge of teacher education and ought to include the same dimensions and aspects which should characterize the learning of children. How can we talk about structure and its virtues without placing our own professional program and teaching under this same challenge? [4]

NATURE OF INTELLIGENCE AND METHODS OF INQUIRY

Without attempting to review all the different concepts of intelligence as innate, environmental, or combinations of these factors, let us accept Guilford's "Three Faces of Intellect" [5] as a model. We need to assume that we do not know the extent to which each factor is determined by heredity or environment and to take the position that every intellectual factor can be developed in individuals, at least to some extent, by learning. If Guilford's structuring of intelligence is valid—and it is supported by considerable evidence—this model should serve as a reference for considering the different kinds of intellectual operations which should have an important part in our educational planning and practices.

Intelligence is classified by Guilford according to the kind of process or operation involved (cognition, memory, convergent thinking, divergent thinking, and evaluation); according to the kind of material or content (figural, symbolic, semantic, and behavioral); and according to the kinds of products (units, classes, relations, systems, transformations, and implications).

---

[4] Virgil E. Herrick, "Teaching as a Set of Curriculum Decisions," paper given at Conference on Teaching, University of Wisconsin, Milwaukee, October 23, 1962.

[5] J. P. Guilford, "Three Faces of Intellect," *American Psychologist*, XIV (August, 1959) pp. 469–79.

We shall not attempt to spend too much time discussing what this model suggests; it seems clear that, of the operations, cognition, memory, and convergent thinking are the ones stressed in most programs of instruction. Divergent thinking and evaluation operations, perhaps, are stressed least; yet studies of creativity stress divergent rather than convergent thinking and evaluation rather than memory. This observation seems to suggest instructional conditions which do not always "zero in" the student to a single generalization, but which would encourage reactions which are seemingly unrelated—reactions that are prized as possible contributions, if not to the point of issue, certainly to other, perhaps equally important ways of perceiving the problem and resolving it. Obviously, many classrooms in all areas of instruction do not provide the conditions which permit divergent and evaluative thinking to take place. They should.

In examining the content dimensions of intelligence, most teachers pay some attention to the figural, symbolic, and semantic contents of the students' learning experience. The point of importance here is that all of these content aspects of intelligence are necessary at every level of the school program. Too often the figural aspects of the learning situation (objects, form, structure, size, and shape) drop out in the latter emphasis on symbols and ideas.

The product dimensions of intelligence—units, classes, relations, systems, transformations, and implications—suggest a line of direction in classroom instruction. The learner should move from a consideration of the nature of the units he uses to observe, manipulate, and perhaps quantify his thinking to a consideration of the nature of the classes, relations, systems, transformation, and implications which would give greater power and quality to his thinking.

This brief use of this model for intelligence suggests the nature of the directions in which we should move in our curriculum planning and instructional programs if we are to bring increasing excellence to the rational thinking of free men. We propose that curricular structures which are more flexible than the many rigid patterns now used or proposed permit and support much more adequately this kind of development.

Bloom's *Taxonomy of Educational Objectives: The Cognitive Domain* [6] can also be used to show the range of intellectual operations representing a possible line of development.

In this study, intellectual abilities and skills are arranged in a continuum of comprehension (lowest level), through application and synthesis, to evaluation (judgments about the value of material and methods for given purposes). Again, it is suggested that our curricular planning consider the full range of these abilities, with a realistic attempt to consider the types of curricular structures and instructional strategies which emphasize the movement in emphasis —that is, from just knowing what is being communicated through application and analysis to synthesizing and the judging of the value of this whole for given purposes.

When the teacher sees her instruction organized about specifics to be learned in rigid ways, with precise limited outcomes, with limited responsibility of the learner to become aware of what is being communicated, then analysis, synthesis, and evaluation are not the intellectual abilities being generated in these classes. The curriculum organization must be established around units sufficiently comprehensive and significant to support these qualities of intellectual behavior. It is as simple as this: limited and restricted instructional organizations do not support broad and vital learnings.

One cannot develop any ability in analysis, synthesis, and evaluation unless an area of study, a problem identified, or a significant question to be answered is observed and studied long enough for such intellectual operations to become a significant part of the learning behavior of the teaching-learning act. You cannot force analysis and evaluation into a single class period and expect students to play a significant role in dealing with these intellectual questions. The unit of instructional planning must be comprehensive enough in nature and in time to permit the rational processes of the student to operate actively on the reorganization and valuing of the ideas and understandings being gained.

---

[6] Benjamin Bloom, ed., *Taxonomy of Educational Objectives: The Cognitive Domain* (New York: David McKay Co., Inc., 1946) 207 pp.

Piaget's work [7] on the stages and the nature of intellectual development is used by many people to justify all kinds of instructional practices and sequence planning. His contribution is more in terms of describing the nature of the child's thinking than it is in identifying precisely the time period when certain qualities of thinking will appear. His work suffers the same weaknesses that Gesell's does when he attempts to describe the stages of growth after five years of age.[8] Piaget's three stages—(1) the preoperational stage (from ages 1-5-6), which lacks the principle of reversibility; (2) the stage of concrete operations (ages 5-10-14), which includes manipulation of objects, both internally and externally); (3) the stage of formal operations, the ability to operate on hypothetical propositions (after 14)—are suggestive again of the range of intellectual operations which ought to be considered in an adequate instructional program. This sequence, at least for a child in school, may be a continuum of quality rather than a sequence in time of development. There is a growing body of evidence to suggest both the validity of Piaget's analysis of the nature of a child's thinking and the invalidity of the implied time sequence. If the character of the education experience is adequate, and if opportunity is provided for a range of intellectual operations to take place, it is likely that children at every level of the common school will exhibit all three stages of intellectual operations to some degree.

Bloom's and Broder's study [9] of the problem-solving processes of college students provides us with some interesting propositions

---

[7] Jean Piaget, *The Language and Thought of the Child* (Cleveland: The World Publishing Company, 1955). The work reported in this printing was done in 1921–22 at the Institut Rousseau and reported in several editions, the last in 1930. The other books by Piaget relevant to this point are *The Child's Conception of the World, The Construction of Reality in the Child*, and *The Psychology of Intelligence*.

[8] Arnold Gesell et al., *The Child from Five to Ten* (New York: Harper & Row, Publishers, 1946) 475 pp.

[9] Benjamin Bloom and Lois J. Broder, *Problem Solving Processes of College Students*, Supplementary Educational Monographs, No. 73 (Chicago: University of Chicago Press, 1950) pp. 1–31.

regarding ways to encourage greater skill in problem-solving. The authors of this study found the major differences between successful and nonsuccessful students in problem-solving had to do with their ability to start the attack on a problem, in the extent to which they could bring relevant knowledge to bear on the problem, in the extent to which their attack was active or passive, in their ability to follow through, and in their general confidence in their ability to solve problems. These groups were not significantly different in ability or in amount of general information known.

These results sharply point up the danger of assuming that ability and knowledge will in themselves be sufficient to assure problem-solving abilities. In curriculum programs where there is a concern about the growing ability of students to solve problems of all kinds, there must first be problems which are worth studying and thinking about. Second, there must be equal attention to the development of useful strategies for attacking problems, the emphasis on active rather than passive involvements by students, the providing of time, facilities, and concern for following through on problem solutions, and finally the continuous concern for and achievement in problem-solving throughout the student's educational experiences. It is this kind of training which will strengthen every student's confidence in his own problem-solving abilities: not programs which place primary emphasis on content and its retention.

Curriculum structures and instructional plans must be examined to see the extent to which the above is considered an important and necessary part of such planning and teaching. Some of us believe that when such structures place high priority on the learner and on persistent and recurring problems of living (or of the content field) as organizing centers, this skill in all its dimensions will be more likely to increase than when more restricted and limited centers are used. We feel, also, that when curriculum structures which pay attention to relating ability, knowledge, and problem-solving skills to the solutions of issues and questions of significance to both individuals and humanity, such education becomes truly liberal.

Recent examinations of creativity add additional support for the general thesis which is emerging from studies on intelligence and the related operations of thinking and problem-solving. The work of Getzels and Jackson [10] at Chicago shows the lack of direct correspondence between "just high I.Q.'s" and high creativity. Torrance's work [11] at Minnesota emphasizes the importance of a climate which allows new ideas to be respected and encouraged, pointing out that any break with accustomed tradition and ways of thinking is always accompanied by serious logical criticisms and attack. In a classroom where propositions and answers are always black and white, where truth is examined primarily on the basis of personal authority, where only one way is considered an appropriate way to deal with the work at hand, and where efforts are made to exert group pressures to create normative conditions for learning, real obstacles to creative thinking as well as to becoming an adequate person are created.

A learner must feel reasonably secure in his social framework if he is to be creative; he needs the sympathetic rapport, not aggressions, of others in his environment, especially those who have power over him—such as his teachers and his peer group. The social and emotional climate and the power structure of a classroom is related to the intellectual and creative life of the student and must not be ignored. Curriculum planning which is concerned with excellence in the realm of the intellect must also be equally concerned with excellence in the realm of humanity, and the aiding of students to achieve their own personal and social self-realization must be considered. There is a suggestion in much of our research that the latter is a necessary and prior consideration for the former.

TEACHER-LEARNER ROLES

As the different areas of controversy in curriculum thinking have been examined, the importance of the role of the teacher and the student in the learning process becomes increasingly

---

[10] Jacob W. Getzels and P. W. Jackson, "The Study of Giftedness; A Multi-Dimensional Approach," *The Gifted Student,* Cooperative Research Monograph No. 2, U.S. Department of Health, Education and Welfare (Washington, D.C.: U. S. Government Printing Office, 1960).

[11] E. Paul Torrance et al., *Assessing the Creative Thinking Abilities of Children,* unpublished monograph (University of Minnesota: Bureau of Educational Research, College of Education, 1960) 192 pp.

apparent. The most important educational experience happening to a student *is his teacher.* Her vision of the world, life, learning, and man limits or broadens, attacks or supports, impoverishes or enriches the educational experiences of every student. Her rigidities or flexibilities in curriculum planning and teaching support or deny the kind of creativity we have been talking about in teaching and program planning. One place where all these aspects come together in concrete form is in her concept of her role and the kind of power or authority this role provides for directing and supporting the teaching-learning act.

A long range of studies of interaction patterns in classroom behavior (Lewin and Lippitt,[12] Anderson and Brewer,[13] Withall,[14] Thelen,[15] B. O. Smith and others,[16] Marie Hughes,[17] and Ned Flanders [18]) point out the critical effect of the teachers' authoritarian-democratic, dominative-integrative, logically clarifying, direct-indirect patterns of behavior both on the quality of the learning outcome and on the quality of the pupils' participation in the learning enterprise.

In the words of Flanders:

. . . it was shown that under controlled conditions, seventh grade English-social studies pupils and eighth grade mathematics students showed greater subject matter achievement when exposed to more

---

[12] K. Lewin, R. Lippitt and Sibylle K. Escalona, "Studies in Topological and Vector Psychology," *Studies in Child Welfare,* Vol. XVI, No. 3 (Iowa City, Iowa: University of Iowa, 1940).

[13] H. H. Anderson and Helen M. Brewer, "Studies of Teachers' Classroom Personalities I, Dominative and Socially Integrative Behavior of Kindergarten Teachers," *Applied Psychology Monographs* (1945) No. 6. Also Studies No. II and III (1946) No. 8 and (1946) No. 11.

[14] John Withall, "Assessment of the Social-emotional Climate Experienced by a Group of Seventh Graders as They Moved From Class to Class," *Educational Psychology Measurement,* XII (1952) pp. 440–51.

[15] Herbert T. Thelen, *Teachability Grouping* (Chicago: University of Chicago Press, 1961).

[16] B. O. Smith, *A Study of the Logic of Teaching* (Urbana, Illinois: Bureau of Educational Research, University of Illinois, 1960).

[17] Marie Hughes, *A Research Report: Assessment of Quality of Teaching in Elementary Schools* (Salt Lake City, Utah: University of Utah, 1959).

[18] Ned Flanders, "A Cross-National Comparison of New Zealand and Minnesota Teacher-Pupil Relationships," mimeographed paper given at A. E. R. A. meetings, February, 1962, Atlantic City, New Jersey, p. 10.

indirect, flexible patterns of teacher influence. In these same experiments scores of pupils on the attitude inventory were correlated between +0.45 and +0.49 with achievement scores adjusted for initial ability. It appears that subject matter achievement, constructive pupil attitudes and the teacher's tendency to use more indirect, flexible patterns of influence are all positively correlated. To the extent that one can accept these interrelationships, the quality of education in Minnesota and New Zealand classrooms can be improved by reducing teacher domination, giving more attention to ideas expressed by pupils, and permitting pupils to have more self-direction through greater freedom of action. Just how much of a shift in the teacher's pattern of influence would help and whether too much of a shift would hinder the quality of education remains to be explored. One way to express our findings is to say that the teachers in low scoring classrooms were willing to work too hard in that they directed and supervised pupil learning activities more closely than was necessary for maximum learning.

The work at Stanford, while supporting Flander's thesis, in general suggests that the distinction between direct and indirect teaching is not completely clear. The results there indicate that indirect, permissive procedures in the preliminary exploration of a problem or area, identification of possible working strategies, and use of resources should be followed by more direct clarification of working plans, objectives to be achieved, resources to be used, responsibilities to be assumed, and due dates to be met. Artistic teaching comes, it seems, when exploration, creativeness, and acceptance are followed by commitment, follow-through, and evaluation based on known goals and norms.

This point is brought out most clearly in our examination of teacher-pupil roles in the evaluation process. Our studies (at the University of Wisconsin) show that if the student is to move toward self-evaluation and constructive direction of future learning behavior, then his roles in the evaluation processes of goal-setting, behavior-defining, observing, norm-setting, judging, and inferring future consequent phases of the evaluation process must be maximized. If self-evaluation and more intelligent future direction of behavior based on such evaluation is not a value, then we should maximize the teacher's role in all phases of the evaluation process. And this is just what we do. This is the nature of the teacher choice we must make if more intelligent self-direction is to occur from our educational programs and teaching processes. We never stand still; golden means have little value; we either move toward or away from the values we hold. If we want intelligent self-direction, then it is clear that the student's role in the evaluation process must be increased. It is impossible for us to remain passive or aloof from this choice; we make it whether we are conscious of it or not. It seems only reasonable, therefore, if we are rational, constructive, responsible men, that we make the choice in a way which will move us toward the goals we all seem to accept.

SUMMARY

This examination of some of the dilemmas in curriculum thinking and planning as they relate to our overarching purposes of education have led to a number of generalizations:

1. Everyone is concerned with excellence, maximum self-realization, and the achievement of a rational man in our times. We differ on what these terms mean and how to achieve this goal.

2. There is more than one base upon which curriculum structures can be erected. Our almost exclusive preoccupation with subject matter gives rise to the danger that we will fall behind in creative, imaginative thinking about the different ways in which an educational program can be planned. It was pointed out that this kind of thinking will improve, not detract from, subject teaching.

3. There is need for more careful examination of what is meant by "subject" and what this implies for curriculum planning. The scope of the curriculum for the present day, for the cold war, or for the future, cannot be limited to the hard subjects.

4. Structures exist and can be developed on any base and are not the private and unique characteristic of subjects. Each subject has more than one way of relating and interpreting its cognitive field. There is value in helping the student discover how to structure his own learning. It is important that teachers know about structure and structuring.

5. Concepts of intelligence and thought processes contribute a great deal to the understanding of the learning process, and there is need to make sure that their cultivation and development become an integral part of the teaching-learning process. There is a growing body of evidence to show the necessary importance of the social-emotional environment within which such thinking takes place. Any attempt to ignore or to negate this aspect of rational behavior is critically to obstruct the intellectual development of children and youth in our schools.

6. The teacher's role in the teaching-learning act is critical. As she moves in the direction of assuming the supporting, clarifying, and facilitating roles in her teaching, the learner tends to maximize his active responsible part in the learning process, and, as a consequence, he not only learns more but also becomes more effective in dealing with his own personal and social needs.

7. The many social forces of our enlarging world, increasing populations, exploding knowledge, technology, shrinking land space, reducing work, and increasing leisure opportunities in the context of international tensions and threat present factors which cannot be ignored in planning both the content and context of our present-day education for free men in a democratic society. Ignoring these forces in our curriculum planning and teaching can only lead to inadequate and dangerous educational programs for our society.

8. There is an obvious need to find a curriculum structure which would include the important and necessary dimensions of an adequate education for free, rational, and responsible men in our society. Such a structure would be as valuable for giving direction to teacher education as it would be for planning programs for elementary and secondary schools. At the present time, subject areas provide the major framework within which we operate.

These problems and issues of curriculum planning and teaching, and some of the directives emerging from present-day research provide major challenges to educators. May we have the vision, courage, and strength to deal with them in ever more constructive and significant ways.

PART TWO

Developing Instructional Theory

What are the major components of instructional theory? How are the operations of establishing objectives, selecting and organizing learning experiences, and evaluating brought together in the teaching-learning act? These questions serve as focal points for the discussion in this section.

Section II is devoted to the postulates on which instructional theory should be based. The first paper establishes the theme of teaching as curriculum decision-making. Each of the major decision areas— objectives, selecting and organizing, and evaluating— is developed in depth in the next three selections. The last two selections in this section demonstrate applications of particular instructional operations to social studies programming and individualized instruction.

D. W. A.
J. B. M.
F. B. M.

5

Teaching As Curriculum Decision-Making

Joseph Schwab in his excellent paper, "Education and the Structure of the Disciplines," [1] *shows the wide differences in experimentation and explanation of the organism by a biologist when there are differences in conception of the organism. When the biologist conceived the organism as "many pairs of fixed and determinate cause-effect connections," this conception led to an attempt to identify the causal factors. When the biologist conceived the organism "as a collection of equilibrium points around each of which a limited degree of variation occurs;" or "as a vastly complicated 'feedback' mechanism in which damage or change in one part would be followed by 'correction' changes in many others," then these conceptions led to quite different approaches and explanation.*

Virgil E. Herrick

---

[1] Joseph J. Schwab, "Education and the Structure of the Disciplines," Parts I and II, a paper prepared for Project on the Instructional Program of the Public Schools, National Education Association, 1201 Sixteenth Street, N.W., Washington 6, D.C., mimeographed 1961, p. 20.

What is true of biologists and the ways in which they have conceived and studied the organism is even more true of educationists and the ways in which we have conceived and studied teaching. Barr,[2] in his final and most comprehensive review of teaching effectiveness and its correlates, identifies and places in context the many different motives and conceptions which have actuated the numerous studies of teaching and teachers over the past half-century of research effort. It is very clear from this review and that of others [3,4] that teaching is conceived in what is emphasized and cherished as being significant in understanding and directing the teaching-learning process. It is clear, also, that we have moved from seeing effective teaching in terms of the qualities and behaviors of the person to considering effectiveness in teaching as the result of the dynamic interactions which exist between a number of vital aspects of the teaching-learning situation and a teacher.

Concepts of teaching which emphasize this later point of view, while borrowing heavily from psychology, sociology, and philosophy for theoretical frameworks, have been concerned with actual classroom situations and with devising categories of behavior which explain and relate the complicated processes of classrooms.

An examination of interaction studies of teaching, for example, has shown a concern for the logical operations involved in clarifying understanding,[5] the sending and receiving acts of the teacher,[6]

---

[2] A. S. Barr et al., *Wisconsin Studies of the Measurement and Prediction of Teacher Effectiveness: A Summary of Investigations* (Madison, Wisconsin: Dembar Publications, Inc., 1961) pp. 134–52.

[3] Arno A. Bellack and Dwayne Huebner, "Teaching," *Review of Educational Research*, Vol. XXX, No. 3 (June 1960) pp. 246–57.

[4] Nathan L. Gage, ed., *Handbook of Research in Teaching*, a project of the American Educational Research Association, N.E.A. (Chicago: Rand McNally & Co., 1963).

[5] B. Othanel Smith et al., *A Study of the Logic of Teaching: A Report on the First Phase of a Five-Year Research Project* (Urbana, Illinois: Bureau of Educational Research, University of Illinois, 1960).

[6] John M. Newell, W. W. Lewis, and John Withall, *Mental Health Teacher Education Research Project* (Madison, Wisconsin: University of Wisconsin, 1960).

the integrative-dominative function of a teacher,[7,8] and the management of teachable groups.[9]

As laudable as it is to study teaching with some appreciation of the complex interactions of the personal, logical, social, and psychological nature which take place in the classroom situation, it is somewhat amazing that the conceptual structures used to analyze these records of classroom behavior have practically ignored many of the curricular operations so important in teaching. Many of the interactions contained in a running record of classroom behavior are influenced or determined by prior or on-the-spot decisions about the important curriculum operations.

The important findings of Anderson,[10] Lippitt,[11] Withall,[12] Flanders,[13] and Hughes, et al.[14] in regard to autocratic-democratic, dominative-integrative, direct-indirect teaching are dependent ultimately on a teacher's choice of a curricular pattern and what this means for her role in respect to the learner as supportive and encouraging rather than dominative and directive. Her curriculum decisions will supply organizing centers which permit or obstruct exploration and progressive goal definition, communication sys-

---

[7] Ned Flanders, *Teacher Influence, Pupil Attitudes and Achievement: Studies in Interaction Analysis* (Minneapolis, Minnesota: University of Minnesota, 1960).

[8] Marie W. Hughes et al., *A Research Report: Assessment of the Quality of Teaching in Elementary Schools* (Salt Lake City, Utah: University of Utah, 1959).

[9] Herbert Thelen, *Teachability Groupings*, a research study conducted under a grant from the cooperative Research Branch, U.S. Office of Education (Chicago: University of Chicago, 1961).

[10] H. H. Anderson and Helen M. Brewer, "Studies of Teachers' Classroom Personalities I, Dominative and Socially Integrative Behavior of Kindergarten Teachers," *Applied Psychology Monographs*, No. 6 (1945). Also Studies No. II and III ((1946) No. 8 and (1946) No. 11.

[11] K. Lewin, R. Lippitt, and Sibylle K. Escalona, "Studies in Topological and Vector Psychology," *Studies in Child Welfare*, Vol. XVI, No. 3 (Iowa City, Iowa: University of Iowa, 1940).

[12] John Withall, "Assessment of the Social-emotional Climate Experienced by a Group of Seventh Graders as They Moved from Class to Class," *Educational Psychology Measurement*, XII (1952) pp. 440-51.

[13] Flanders, *op. cit.*

[14] Hughes et al., *op. cit.*

tems which permit or obstruct meaning clarification, role clarifications which encourage or deny responsibility and constructive participation in the learning act by all concerned. The psychological and social parallelism of "autocratic-democratic" "dominative-integrative," "direct-indirect" can be matched and associated with similar curricular parallelisms as "subject-centered child-centered, fact-centered problem-centered," and "deductive-inductive" instructional planning and teaching. The psychological, social, and curricular referents are not unrelated dimensions in teaching, but should be a clear and necessary part of any over-all framework which places each in its proper context. It is merely proposed here that the curricular decisions necessary to permit and give significant direction to any psychological and social choice of democratic, integrative, and indirect patterns of classroom instruction should be a part of any adequate concept of teaching.

THE COMPONENTS OF AN ADEQUATE FRAMEWORK FOR TEACHING

In thinking about what constitutes an adequate framework for teaching, it is useful to ask again the earlier question, "What are the necessary components of teaching?" One needs to know what is involved or what kind of categories of things one must deal with in any adequate concept of teaching. Answers to this question provide one with one class of referents for building a curriculum theory.

Since much of our thinking about teaching has focused on the teacher in her classroom, it is useful to keep this vantage point and consider the question of the components of teaching. With this focus it is possible to identify the following aspects of teaching.

Different classes of objects

Three classes of objects are found in the teaching situation.

Class One. Dynamic, purposive human beings. Humans having a personality, goal perceptions, and a self-concept.

Humans can be further divided into four levels of relationship to the teaching act: (a) teacher and learners directly involved; (b) principal, supervisors, janitor, etc., who usually operate in a secondary relationship; (c) parents and other adults having primary relationship to a child; (d) other adults concerned with education.

Class Two. Objects devised to contain and develop educational programs—frequently highly self-contained. Textbooks, workbooks, films and film strips, teaching machine programs.

Class Three. Objects not specifically designed to convey educational programs—chairs, desks, tables, pictures, blocks.

Objects have unitary characteristics, occupy space, and can be selected for various purposes and arranged in various physical patterns. Usually, too, these objects have implicit functions of their own which may or may not be consistent with their selected educational function in the classroom.

A geographic space and structure

Teaching always takes place somewhere and demands space and some arrangement of objects in this space. The nature and amount of geography available or used for teaching obviously is a factor. Grouping and classification of pupils are frequently geography problems, and every teaching plan has a geographic dimension of time, space, and physical structure.

A social space and structure

Many studies of group dynamics and the sociology of the classroom have concerned themselves with the social structure and climate of classroom behavior. Perhaps the most important part of the social structure of a classroom is its power structure and the related authority or prestige roles played by teachers and students. A third factor to consider in the social space and structure of a classroom is that it exists in relation to other social systems which make up a school and its related social communities.

A communication system with appropriate signs and symbols

It is clear that one of the most important aspects of teaching is its communication system. Both child and teacher have to learn its nature and uses in the educational process.

An educational structure

The overriding structure of a classroom is the educational plan or program with its objectives, curricular areas, teaching plans, and instructional strategies. It is this all-inclusive structure which should encompass the other components of the classroom and give them meaning and function.

Important dimensions

In each of the above necessary components, a number of important dimensions are found—the dimensions of feeling, of ideas and related cognitive processes, and of value.

These dimensions need a location and necessary referents to make them meaningful and available for study and modification. It is futile to deal with them as unique units of teaching because of this dependent quality.

This list, I am sure, can be improved and better structured, but it is valuable for our purpose in that it identifies some of the things which are always present in every act of teaching, good or bad, irrespective of any concept of instruction and regardless of where the act takes place. This list helps explain, too, why many of the researchers on teaching have attempted to seize on one or a limited combination of these components—teacher, child, social system, cognitive domain, teaching plan—for their research targets, and they thereby assumed that this target was sufficient in itself to explain and predict teaching.

THE CRITERIA FOR AN ADEQUATE
FRAMEWORK OF TEACHING

The above conception of the components of the classroom teaching-learning situation is based on the following assumptions:

(1) that teaching is a complex, multidimensioned act; (2) that it is concerned primarily with the efficient achievement of educational objectives; (3) that it involves the responsible decision-making and action of a teacher; and (4) that it can take place in different kinds of social-physical settings and can be directed by different educational rationales.

In view of these assumptions of the teaching-learning situation, what are the criteria for an adequate framework for teaching? It is proposed that an adequate framework for teaching must be:

1. Comprehensive in the sense that it includes and finds a place for all other subsystems important in teaching.

2. More than a research rationale. Must be *developmental* in the sense that it permits going behind the specific teaching act to the phases of conceptualizing, structuring, acting, evaluating, and programming by both teacher and pupil.

3. Open-ended, nonvaluing, and reasonably nonstructured, but must permit supplying many different valuing structures and rationales to its framework, leading to many specific answers and plans for teaching consistent with such value orientations.

4. Meaningful in relation to general education and the foundational areas for teaching. It should serve as a means for forming a unified structure of knowledge and values about life and education, as well as about teaching, and curriculum planning.

5. Utilizing high face validity for dealing with both the act of teaching and the study and development of our metaknowledge about how to plan and deal with the teaching act more effectively.

A PROPOSED FRAMEWORK

It should be clear to everyone that we are not in a position to say with confidence that we have a framework for teaching which would meet all of these criteria. We do feel, however, that such a framework should be organized around the common operations of curriculum and instruction. These operations provide the important connecting points for the valuing structures and form the referents for the important curricular and instructional decisions made by anyone dealing with the teaching-learning act. These operations have high face validity, are open-ended, relatively nonstructured, and can be used to relate the contributions of general education as well as the foundational areas of education to the teaching act.

It is important to note that prior commitments to curricular patterns exist in varying degrees of completeness to form the general context within which the specific planning and action of the classroom takes place.

Another important point is that the planning and designing functions are a part of the specific curricular operations of the teaching act. There is no such thing as an unplanned curriculum or incidental teaching. There are only two planning alternatives open to a teacher: either she knows, in general, the curriculum pattern she will use, or she knows the way in which such plans are developed with children.

The following operations are proposed as the broad reference points for curriculum planning and for teaching. This listing does not imply any significant ordering or structuring. It should be clear to any teacher that always to begin with purposes and end with evaluation in every teaching act would not be practical.

1. *The operations involved in goal-setting, objective-determining, or determination of outcome.*

It should be clear to curriculum researchers who have studied a wide array of classroom records that few teachers start their planning with a set of instructional objectives. They are much more likely to start with topics, objects, or a section of a textbook as an initial step. Then, this topic or story is examined to see what important outcomes may grow out of its study. Frequently, in this latter case, the learner assumes a responsible role for identification and statement of outcomes. Of course, it is clear that, classically, it is possible to start with objectives and then proceed to a consideration of the learning experiences which will enable children to perceive and understand them.

An important part of the goal-setting operations of curriculum is the realization by the teacher that a necessary aspect of any set of objectives deals with the intellectual, social, and communication processes important in learning and education. This realization and use of such objectives to plan and structure teaching operations will make a great difference in the nature of the teacher-student interaction observed and recorded in such studies. Again, it is argued that this kind of curricular perception is a prior and necessary consideration by a teacher or research worker in any attempt to understand and to deal with the teaching act effectively.

When a teacher assumes a responsibility for developing effective methods of inquiry in addition to important concepts, then her curriculum planning must be the kind which selects organizing centers which will permit observation, experimentation, and testing of hypotheses. This commitment will lead to teaching structures which will encourage certain kinds of questions, patterns of teacher-student interaction, and learning roles assumed by students. When teachers do not see these process objectives as important, different teaching patterns and behaviors tend to follow.

2. *Operations involved in the selection and evaluation phases of curriculum planning and teaching.*

Every important curriculum operation involves the making of choices and evaluations by those who are involved. When a teacher is considering the nature of the question she is going to ask to start a given lesson, her choice is based on a consideration of the kind of objectives to be achieved, the kind of object, topic, or problem to be developed, and the direction in which the learning action might move, as well as her assessment of the children, their interests, and their backgrounds. If her teaching conception includes the importance of maximizing the role and responsibility of the learner in the making of choices and in the evaluation of consequences, then it is very likely that the nature of classroom interactions will be very different from what they would be if the teacher's conception were that these selection and evaluation procedures were primarily her function as the key figure in such decision-making, or worse, if her choice were made by the nature of the instructional materials she is using.

The examination of classroom episodes shows that many of the teacher's acts are concerned with reinforcing and giving cues to the direction she wishes the class to take or to the shutting off of avenues of discussion and exploration which seem to be leading away from the central topic or purpose. These boundary- and direction-determining functions are based on selection and evaluation procedures and may be the exclusive responsibility of the teacher, or they may involve the student in varying degrees of responsibility and control. If this latter is true, then the teacher increasingly moves to a consideration with the students of how such decisions should be made and how the students can use this kind of understanding to deal with similar problems in the future. Again, this kind of curriculum conception and decision-making will result in interaction patterns which will differ in significant ways from those of a teacher who holds a different concept of teacher-student roles in decision-making.

Many of the studies of teaching have made much of the authority figure and normative behavior of the teacher in the teaching act. The curricular parallelism relates to the operations in evaluation and the nature of the part the teacher plays in it. Playing one role, she becomes the authority figure and assumes much of the dominative behavior associated with this role. Playing another role in this same process, she assumes much of the integrative and supporting behavior associated with a different teaching pattern.

Again, it is the thesis here that an understanding of the important components of the curricular evaluation operations would place both of these roles in the same context and would explain the resulting differences.

For example, the essential aspects of evaluation include: (1) identified objectives; (2) the definition of these objectives in terms of behaviors which would characterize them; (3) a set of observations of the behavior of individuals being evaluated in appropriate situations; (4) the development of criteria for determining the degree of adequacy of observed behavior; (5) the valuing of these behaviors in the light of the identified objectives and in relation to the criteria or norms; and (6) the use of these evaluations in determining and directing future behavior.

In relation to these aspects of evaluations a number of roles can be played: the role of the individual being observed and judged, of the determiner of the objectives and their definition, of the observer, of the determiner of the norms or criteria of adequacy, of the judger of the acts being observed, and finally, of the individual who uses these evaluations to direct his future actions. It is clear that a single individual must play all these roles in self-evaluation. It is clear also that, in most teaching, the teacher is the goal and norm determiner and definer, and the observer and the appraiser of the action. All the learner does is to behave according to goals unknown to him, to be judged on bases unavailable for his present and future use, and to direct his future behavior toward equally unknown educational objectives.

It is possible, therefore, to develop a particular curricular-evaluation model for the normative and authority roles played by teachers in the array of teacher interaction studies by identifying the roles the teacher or student plays in dealing with the necessary dimensions of the evaluation process. The use of any of these curricular-evaluation models by a teacher would direct and differentiate her teaching behavior and communication systems in this area of the teaching process. From this point of view, also, an acceptant and supportive teacher is one who helps a student distinguish his own sense of value from his behavior related to his achievement of educational goals and permits their evaluation on constructive educational norms rather than on punitive and personal bases. This is merely another kind of curricular-evaluation model for dealing with the evaluation dimensions of the teaching-learning act. It is proposed, therefore, that our conception of teaching should include a consideration of these operations and the nature of the understandings and decisions which will result in more educationally valid evaluation models and, consequently, more educationally valid teaching behavior.

3. *Operations involved in organizing curriculum components into educational structures and teaching patterns.*

The decisions related to organizing and developing learning experiences with children form the central focus for all curriculum and teaching operations. Decisions concerning objectives, evaluations, and over-all orientations have their ultimate consequence in what one does about organizing and developing the teaching act with children.

Three decision areas may be identified in the organizing operations. These decision areas are (1) determining what is involved; (2) selecting organizing centers; and (3) determining the continuity or sequence dimension. Obviously, these decision points are not unrelated, and certain decisions made in area one provide the basic working materials for dealing with decisions in areas two and three.

The decision of what is involved

This question is seldom discussed in books on curriculum, but examination of curriculum plans and teaching episodes reveals that the way in which this question is perceived and answered limits and directs the way in which the teaching-learning act is organized.

On one level of curriculum decision-making, this question is illustrated by a teacher's considering how she is going to deal with the topic of weather. One way of considering weather is to see it as being composed of air mass and its movement, temperature and its source, and moisture and its sources. One test of the adequacy of this conception of the necessary components of weather is to consider the question that if one could control the movement of air, temperature, and moisture, would it be possible to create the kind of weather one would want? In whatever way one would answer this question, it should be clear that this conception of essential components would furnish the kinds of phenomena to observe, the conditions to be related, and possible organizational patterns to be considered in any teaching about weather.

On a more general level, if one sees social studies as dealing fundamentally with human relationships, including such dimensions as common and persistent problems of living, social processes for dealing with such problems, geographic, political, and social areas within which these problems occur, subject matter about these aspects, and the tools and skills of social inquiry and analysis, then this array of components provides the building blocks for organizing and structuring social studies programs and teaching. If one starts with political or geographic areas as the important organizational reference, then this approach leads to a different way of organizing social studies than if one sees the common and reoccurring problems of living as the fundamental organizing elements. This follows also if the subject matter and its major organizing generalizations were used as the major organizing base. The point here is that the selection of a particular aspect of social studies as the major organizing referent leads to different organizing structures, but that each structure would include all of the necessary components at some point. This same proposition can be illustrated by using conceptions of necessary components for the language arts, mathematics, and science.

The decisions about the organizing centers[15]

Our study of teaching episodes indicates that one of the key decisions a teacher makes has to do with the organizing centers used to start and develop the lesson. The decision as to the kind of organizing center selected has a great deal to do with the way individual differences are handled and how more than one child is included in the teaching-learning act.[16]

Decisions regarding patterns of relationships and sequence in organization.

A number of structures and continuities are possible in every lesson or class taught by a teacher. The selection of a given one will permit the understanding and participation of students in its development or it will restrict and obstruct such participation and seeing of relationships and consequences.

A common sequence is merely the arrangement of limited learning episodes in time and physical proximity to each other. Other more promising continuity structures use such organizing themes as common and persistent problems of living as a basis for moving from one geographic area to another, from one culture to another, and from one time to a past or future. Other centers for developing teaching-learning structures are common geographic characteristics, continuing operations, and key organizing concepts. Illustrations of organization centers which are limited in continuity and organizing possibilities are people, great documents, specific geographic areas, specific cities, political areas, objects of specific character, and the like. Similar analyses of permissive or restrictive organizing centers can be made in each content field.

4. *Operations involved in placing curriculum plans into action.*

It should be recognized that curriculum planning and teaching are a part of the same action pattern. Planning prior to the

---

[15] An organizing center is the point where all the important aspects of the teaching act can be related and given focus.

[16] Virgil E. Herrick, "Curriculum Decisions and Provisions for Individual Differences," *The Elementary School Journal*, LXII, No. 6 (March, 1962) pp. 313–20.

teaching act provides the rationale and framework within which teaching takes place. In the interaction between the teacher, students, and the centers of attention and related feedbacks, changes always take place in the direction, pacing, depth, relationship patterns, continuity, and degree of involvement factors. It is here argued that the thoughtful consideration of the key operations and related decisions in planning of the teaching act by the teacher and, increasingly, by the students is the context in which teaching must be considered and improved.

SUMMARY

This paper has argued for teaching seen as a set of curriculum decisions dealing with important operations of the teaching-learning act. An attempt has been made to describe the criteria which should be met by an adequate framework for understanding and improving teaching. A number of curricular operations are described and examined to show the extent to which decisions made in dealing with these operations would limit and direct the teaching act. It is claimed that, on the basis of the analysis of a wide number of learning episodes, the curriculum decisions made in these episodes account for the interaction patterns, teacher-learner roles, and continuity structure found there.

A framework such as the one proposed here is sufficiently comprehensive to include in some meaningful fashion all the complex elements of teaching in a way that provides the teacher on all levels of professional competence with a powerful tool for skillful action and professional growth. This framework assumes that there are always better answers to be made to these persistent and common operations of all education, teaching, and living. This concept demands all the best contributions of our knowledge, all the directives of our important values, and, best of all, frees the intelligence and creativity of the teacher and student to achieve more significant and vital learning for themselves and for others. Any concept of teaching which, irrespective of the importance of its specialized concern, does less than this is inadequate to give form and direction to the program of teacher education of the universities and colleges of this land.

6

Establishing And Using Objectives

Objectives do not solve all the problems of developing significant educational programs for children, but they do have some very definite jobs to perform. In this selection the author focuses attention upon the ways of considering objectives, the function of objectives, the statement of objectives, and the definition of objectives.

D. W. A.
J. B. M.
F. B. M.

WAYS OF CONSIDERING OBJECTIVES

The words "aims," "goals," "purposes," and "outcomes," as well as "objectives" are found in the literature. We group all of these terms under the general heading of objectives and recognize that the same objective may exist on different levels of generality and specificity without going to the trouble of calling one an "over-all goal" and the other an "aim." In this broad sense, an objective gives direction to behavior, but is never consumed in it.

A second way of looking at objectives is in terms of the various uses of objectives in instruction. Contrary to most teachers' conception, objectives have more uses than serving on an educational masthead. Objectives serve as one of the important definers of scope, provide the initial base for selecting possible learning activities, and form one of the major referents for evaluation. In spite of many attempts to use them as such, objectives should not serve as an organizing center for instruction. Objectives justify their educational existence by the difference they make in what teachers and learners do.

The value of this way of looking at objectives is to point out that a prior and perhaps more important role for objectives to serve, in addition to evaluation, is their role as a basis for identifying and helping select desirable learning activities. It also suggests that a form of definition of a given objective appropriate for selecting learning experiences may not be the same as the form most appropriate for evaluation. Perhaps the same objective will need to be defined in different ways, depending on the use made of the objective.

A third way of looking at objectives is to examine the scope of considerations involved in their development, ranging from a consideration of their source, identification, selection, statement, definition, to considerations of their use. Notwithstanding the great importance of the background for determining a particular set of instructional objectives, this paper focuses only on the problems. of the statement and definition of an objective for evaluation purposes, and is assuming that these other aspects have been adequately treated.

A fourth way of considering objectives is to examine their roles in different curriculum structures. For the purpose of this paper, however, the form of the curriculum structure having subject matter as its major orientation is the only one considered because of its common use. It is well to point out, however, that no other approach to curriculum design makes the same use of objectives as does the subject curriculum. The major importance of this point for this paper is that it is generally agreed that in this way of looking at curriculum, the major concepts and intellectual skills of a given body of subject matter should form the objectives. Objectives of content and process are thus a part of every adequate teaching-learning situation and, therefore, must be considered as necessary related parts of every evaluative situation in school. We need to consider both objectives of content and process from the point of view of their definitions and use in evaluations. The most obvious lesson this point has for present evaluation procedures is to show how much attention we are paying to objectives of content and how little to objectives of process. Further, it is almost unknown in any appraisal technique to consider them both in relation to their necessary roles in the same learning experience. Yet, this is exactly the task curriculum sets for any adequate evaluation procedure in instruction.

THE FUNCTION OF OBJECTIVES

Objectives define the direction of educational development

Objectives, as we have indicated, are the important value statements of what the learner is trying to accomplish or what the educational program is trying to achieve. The first important function of objectives, therefore, is to serve as a statement of the values which help distinguish good educational behavior from bad. Objectives, in this sense, define the nature of the educational maturities that children, teachers, parents, and society are striving to achieve. Objectives form the basis upon which one distinguishes between learning as such and learning which results in education. That learning which results in development related to or moving toward educational objectives constitutes *education.* That learning which results in development opposed to or moving away from educational objectives constitutes *miseducation.* Objectives in this sense are definers of direction and are not ends in themselves. Objectives are not consumed in the process of learning, but they have the capacity for illuminating all learning. Objectives are not things to be mastered, but values whose characteristics can always be incorporated into the behavior of children to some degree. They cannot become the specific learning tasks of the classroom, but they emerge from them as valued learning products.

Objectives help select desirable learning experiences

A second function of objectives is to serve as the major basis upon which children and teachers select desirable learning experiences. This second function of objectives derives itself from the first. If one knows he is trying to build a boat rather than a workbench, that he is trying to go to Milwaukee rather than to Montreal, that he is writing a letter of application for a position rather than a weekly news letter to his grandmother, then he is in a better position to know the kind of lumber, route, and paper he will need, the kind of tools to use, the things to do and say, and the nature and degree of the social and quality standards to apply. Without this knowledge of purpose or goal, learning lacks both direction and efficiency.

This does not mean that a child or a teacher always knows precisely the specific goals being achieved in any learning enterprise, or that all learning activities are selected on the basis of knowing these objectives in advance. The teacher, at times having definite objectives in mind, selects and limits the learning experiences in accordance with this known purpose. At other times, the ongoing enterprise which involved a trip to the firehouse is examined carefully to see what kind of information, understanding, abilities, and attitudes need to grow out of this experience in order to exploit its educational potential to the fullest and to help children to deal more effectively with similar situations in the future. What is important here is to recognize that whether objectives are known in advance or are seen more clearly as a given learning experience develops, both children and teachers must come to some agreement as to what is being accomplished. We must also make certain that the relationship of the things children are doing to these purposes is clearly established in the minds of children.

Although objectives are an extremely important tool for teachers and children to use in selecting the things they need to do in order to accomplish these desired goals, it should be clearly recognized that no one, especially teachers and administrators working with elementary school children, should conceive of them as being the only tool or basis for determining learning activities of a desirable educational program. Other and perhaps equally important bases or screens for selecting learning activities are (1) the plan for ordering or arranging the continuity or sequence of learning over a day, week, school year, or series of grades; (2) the children themselves and their experiences, velocities of development, and ways of learning; and (3) the educational resources of the teacher, school, and community.

It should be recognized here, also, that the statement of the objective should not serve as the direct means for teaching or learning. When this happens, the teacher is having children memorize such concepts as "Air exerts pressure," "A noun is a naming word," "Columbus is the capital of Ohio," and "Receive is spelled r-e-c-e-i-v-e." In this kind of teaching, one is not dealing with the essence of the objective but with the specific means by which the objective is achieved. The possible means by which behavior is influenced should be conceived on a broad basis and should be distinguished from the ends towards which such behavior should move. Important concepts, abilities, and attitudes are internalized within the understanding and behavior of children and must grow out of their experiences; they cannot be memorized and verbalized as things in themselves. The objectives, when they grow out of their experiences and become a part of children's understanding and behavior, help them to become increasingly able to manage and direct their own lives and learning.

Objectives help define the scope of an educational program

A difficult problem of teaching and learning which confronts any teacher and group of children or any curriculum developer is that of knowing the number of different important things that should be considered at a given time. Life, as well as the experiences children have in school, does not have a single unitary characteristic—one thing to look at, to know, or to do something about. Life and the experiences children have in school always present them with a number of things to consider, to select from, to relate, and to act upon. A child and the teacher are always dealing with a number of different possibilities at a given time and, similarly, a child is always learning a number of different things from a single experience.

This important characteristic of all learning and of all educational programs is called *scope, breadth, range,* or more recently, the *horizontal continuity of learning.* All these different terms refer fundamentally to this characteristic of determining the number of different important elements to be considered at a given time in an educational program. The objectives of a school or of a given lesson form one of the important definitions of what the scope of any program or learning experience should be. The ideal is to include all the essential attributes of a desirable elementary school program in the statement of objectives and leave out those which are not essential. This ideal is something very easy to express, but very difficult to accomplish.

The use of a list of objectives as one of the important tools in defining the necessary scope of an educational program or learning experience leads to a number of directives for teaching and evaluation in the elementary school.

First, a community, a staff of a school, or a teacher with children faces the problem of whether or not an educational program includes all of the significant and essential elements of a good education. The statement of objectives is one of the concrete and specific answers to this problem at any particular time and should be an honest, realistic definition of what that program or learning experience is actually trying to achieve.

Second, if a statement of objectives provides a definition of the number of different important aspects of a good learning experience or educational program, then any appraisal or evaluation of that program should consider *all* of these aspects in any judgment of the adequacy of that program. Too often an elementary school is judged adequate or inadequate solely on the basis of concern or lack of concern for phonics, spelling, or handwriting, without any consideration for other aspects of an adequate educational program.

Third, every teacher will want to capitalize on the fact that any learning experience developed with a group of children will always contribute to more than one objective. Economy and efficiency in teaching often comes from exploiting to the fullest the objective developing potential of a limited number of experiences. This has important implications for teaching and curriculum development.

Fourth, every teacher will want to recognize that the educational scope of any learning experience should include possibilities for the development of facts, concepts, or understandings (content); important skills and abilities (processes); and attitudes (values). She will want to exploit the potential of that experience to develop all three.

Fifth, every teacher will want to realize that while objectives are one important definition of *scope,* there are other significant definitions of scope, too: the nature of the experience, problem, topic, or object being considered, and the capacity of a child to perceive and hold a number of different things in some kind of relationship.

Objectives help define the emphasis to be made in an educational program

A list of the objectives for an educational program may define the different necessary components of an adequate educational program, but still not indicate the nature of the emphasis to be made in order to give proper balance and focus to the program of instruction. In general, the same basic objectives give direction to all levels of the educational program of the elementary school. Still, the kindergarten and primary grades emphasize the initial developments of languages, motor behavior, number concepts, and one's understanding of one's self and immediate expanding social and physical environment more than do the middle and upper grades. Similarly, the work of the middle grades tends to emphasize the study and development of areas of living and of understanding more remote from the child's immediate existence in time, space, culture, and his level of generalization. It is not likely, for example, that writing business letters or the problem of choosing a vocation should be emphasized unduly with primary children, whereas the high school and college student would be much more concerned with this kind of problem.

Notwithstanding the importance of this problem of balance and emphasis in educational objectives, not much help is given to the teachers and staffs by the professional literature. It is our feeling that no listing of a number of objectives is adequate to indicate the nature of the emphasis to be made in an educational program at a particular time. Increasingly, objectives will be defined with more than one dimension being used to show this emphasis. Further, it is likely that the nature of the proper emphasis in a list of objectives is not determined by studying objectives, but by studying children and their emerging patterns of development in particular social settings. It is difficult to see how the emphasis and the degree of development possible at a particular time can be determined by the listing of an appropriate direction of objectives in learning. This can only come from the study of the learner and of the social environment in which he exists.

Objectives form one of the major bases for evaluation

Without knowledge of the objectives of an educational program it is impossible to judge its adequacy. All evaluations of human behavior are made in terms of some definition of what is considered important to achieve. Objectives provide this definition and thus form a major basis for the appraisal of the educational development of children. This function is one of the important reasons for communities, teachers, and children to have available a statement of objectives to give direction to and appraise the value of the educational experiences children have in school. Evaluation, reporting, and promotion programs in the elementary school are dependent on the availability of a statement of objectives. Without objectives, such programs can only operate on expediency and on the basis of judgments whose educational bases are unknown.

THE STATEMENTS OF OBJECTIVES

The value of knowing how to state objectives is that a good statement helps everyone concerned to get to what is to be evaluated as quickly as possible. The teacher wanting to state her instructional objectives in a way which could facilitate their use will find the following suggestions helpful.

The statement of objectives should be in terms of the important concepts and processes (abilities) of the subject area or topic being considered.

Illustrations: A number may express a quantity or a relationship (arithmetic). Man depends on other men for many of his needs (social studies). Air has weight (science). To sense a complete thought (language art). To develop critical thinking (general).

Common errors

Restating the need for objectives as an objective. Here teachers and curriculum workers state as their objective, "To teach the important understandings and skills of listening." Nothing is accomplished by this statement other than to repeat you are going to do something about listening. The objectives should be the actual understandings and skills important in this area of the language arts.

Stating a topic or area of study as an objective. Examples of this error would be "to teach addition," "to teach the home," ". . . air," ". . . the predicate nominative," ". . . the New England states," or ". . . transportation." In this way any one of the countless topics, subject subdivisions, objects of science, or phenomena of human behavior would become an objective. These topics or areas of study become very useful definitions of scope for identifying the specific objectives of content and process.

Stating the instructional method as a part of the objective. Under the compulsion of wanting one's instructional objectives to become as inclusive as the total instructional program and thus obstructing the capacity of an objective to do its several jobs well, many curriculum committees and teachers have included objectives such as the following in their lists: "To base instruction in arithmetic on primary and concrete experiences with numbers." "To provide experiences in business uses of arithmetic through audio-visual materials and use of community resources." "To drill on 100 combinations in addition and subtraction." It is very important for a teacher to consider her instructional method and materials at the appropriate time and place. This "time and place" is not when she is trying to state her instructional objectives. "Primary and concrete experiences," "business uses," and "audio-visual materials and community resources," should not appear in statements of objectives, primarily because "means are not ends."

Objectives are used more easily for their purpose if they include only one major referent.

Two objectives in one long involved statement which has more than one major idea or ability is difficult to use because of lack of clarity in the referent. No one knows which one of the several important concepts is being considered in a given instance. Illustrations of this practice are "Large river systems develop in areas of heavy rainfall, and boats carry people and goods from one place to another." "To develop an understanding and appreciation of the home and to teach the care of pets."

Stating the same objective more than once in different words. Most lists of objectives are longer than they should be, primarily because they usually contain the same objective stated more than once, either in different words or on different levels of generality.

Examples

Confusion in level	To develop an understanding in addition. To develop an understanding of 100 additional combinations.
Confusion in words	To develop the understandings of the number system. To develop the basic concepts of number.

Statements of objectives are more useful if they are confined to broad concepts and processes. One of the difficult problems of most teachers in dealing with objectives is to know what to dignify as an objective. A teacher is confronted with the tremendous array of specific factual information and particular skills, all of which seem essential to a well-rounded education for children. So she sees as her instructional objectives the learning of the individual letters of the alphabet, all of the thousands of combinations in arithmetic, the names of the colors, days of the week, months of the year, products of each country, and the like. It is obvious to everyone that education on this level is hopeless.

A more constructive concept of objectives would cause one to look beyond concepts of the fact or of the event to generalizations of relationships and of cause and effect. This latter kind of concept deals with more than one kind of specific and is of importance in dealing with future events of the same kind.

In the following couplets of objectives, the second moves in the direction of being a more important concept to dignify as an objective:

1. (a) Soil, water, and air are natural sources. (b) Any natural substance used to meet a human need is called a natural resource.

2. (a) To develop an ability to put one's hat and coat in his locker. (b) To develop an ability to care for materials and things properly.

3. (a) To recognize the name of each letter. (b) To understand the meaning of the word.

4. (a) A circle is five inches around. (b) The circumference of a circle equals D.

If the above point is valid, then attempts to get sets of unique objectives for a given grade are ill-advised. A more useful attempt could be to identify those concepts and abilities which are important throughout the years of the common school. The degree of understanding of the concepts should be determined by the learner, not the curriculum maker. This point of view, if an adequate one, would have real implications for evaluation procedures.

Statements of objectives are better if unnecessary words and phrases are left out. Common phrases found in many statements of objectives are "to teach," "to help every child learn." Leave these phrases out of the statement of the objectives; they are unnecessary. If the idea needs to be expressed, then make one introductory statement to this effect and leave it out of each subsequent objective.

Many teachers direct the address of their objectives to either the teacher or the child. From the point of view of an objective's usefulness in dealing with curriculum functions, it does not make any difference to whom it is addressed. It is more important that the essential concept of ability be stated as simply and as completely as possible than to worry about who is going to use it. If in doubt, address it to the teacher.

A second group of trouble words in the statement of objectives are adjectives and adverbs dealing with value. To say that a concept is "important," "essential," or "basic" does not make it so.

The valuing process must take place in the identification and selection of the objective, not in its statement. The *nature* of the concept being stated determines its significance, not any value words attached to it. Common examples of such protestation are the following: "To teach the essential and significant concepts of science." "To encourage the development of right personal and social habits of health, courtesy, and kindness in the home." [1]

THE DEFINITION OF OBJECTIVES

To state an objective does not mean that its meaning and essential ramifications are seen clearly by either the person stating the objective or the person using it. Greater confidence that this is true is gained when a definition is made of an objective. Many of the above difficulties in the statement of objectives would be eliminated through the process of definition. In fact, the writer urges curriculum groups not to spend very much time in polishing their fine statements but to move rather rapidly to the process of definition. This process, with its own checks and balances, soon refines and verifies the statement without much difficulty. There is no trouble in recognizing duplication and overlapping when each objective is defined. "Weasel (value and degree) words" stand out.

Three methods of definition have been proposed for objectives. The first method is what we call definition in terms of *essential components*. One must have this type of definition of the objective in hand before the behavioral definition can be accomplished.

The second method of definition has been called the *operational* definition of an objective. This method is particularly appropriate in defining abilities or process objectives, where the operations involved can be distinguished. Actually, this is a behavioral definition, where the operational referent is the element of the process,

---

[1] It is our position that (1) the *value* of an objective has already been established before its statement, and (2) the *degree* to which an objective is achieved is determined, not by any statement or definition of an objective, but by the behavior of the learner and by the norms used to judge the adequacy of this behavior. These norms are not a part of the statement of the objective.

not the learner. Frequently by changing a few words the steps essential in critical thinking can become the "thinking" behaviors of the learner.

The third method of definition, and the one most frequently advocated for evaluation purposes, is to define the objective *behaviorally*, i.e., to describe how the behavior of the learner would characterize his understanding or skill in the area of behavior determined by the objective. Today in curriculum books, the behavioral definition is apparently the only respectable way for an objective to be defined.

The three methods of definition can be seen in the relations to each other shown in Fig. 5.

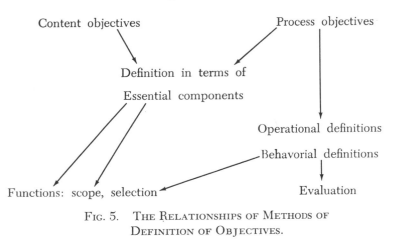

FIG. 5.   THE RELATIONSHIPS OF METHODS OF
DEFINITION OF OBJECTIVES.

There is no question that a behavioral definition of an objective is very useful for evaluation purposes, for it points directly to "behavior to observe" or to test items. It is proposed, however, that these behaviorial definitions are better made when there has been a previous curricular definition of the essential components of the objective.

Definition in terms of the essential components of an objective

Objective: Differences in temperature influence how people live.

Careful examination of this objective reveals that key aspects have to "do with temperature" and with "how people live." The essential aspects of this objective have to do with:

  I. Heat and its relation to temperature
    A. Source of heat
      1. Sun
      2. Fire
      3. Hot substances
    B. Intensity
      1. Nearness to source of heat
      2. Degree of heat
        a. Reference points
          (1) Freezing of water
          (2) Boiling of water
        b. Scales for measuring
      3. Conductors—nonconductors
        a. Media through which heat rays pass
        b. Surface upon which heat rays strike
  II. Heat and its influence on substances
    A. Live objects (bacteria)
    B. Material objects
  III. Effect of differences of heat on aspects of life
    A. Methods of observing temperature and its difference over time
      1. Through man's direct reactions and judgment based on experience
      2. Through instruments—thermometers
    B. Factors of life considered
      1. Personal comfort
      2. Food
      3. Shelter
      4. Clothing
  IV. Situations in which to observe
    A. Situations in child's own experience
    B. People in characteristic climatic regions

There is no brief for the form of this analysis, but a definition of the nature, source, and transmission of heat is the background to examination of the effect of differences of heat on how people live. Some would argue that the following definition would be enough:

Effect of degree of hotness or coldness on personal comfort, food, clothing, shelter.[2]

Definition in terms of operations relating to an objective

The intent behind an operational definition is to identify what needs to be done in order to insure accomplishment. Many times we do not know the answers, but we do know what questions to ask and get answers to in order to solve the problem. An operational definition is much like this: The teacher approaching the task of defining this objective operationally would see that this particular objective has two major parts: "Differences in temperature" and "influences how people live."

I. *Need:* a restrictive definition of the aspects of people's living to consider in relation to differences in temperature.
Possibilities: food, clothing, shelter, communication, transportation, governing, recreating, education.
Criteria of choice
   A. Which of these best shows the influence of temperature on man's living?
   B. Which of these have greatest significance in the eyes of children?
   C. Which of these have greatest transference value to other aspects of man's living? To future, more adult experiences?
   D. Which of these are most accessible and possible to observation and study?

II. *Need:* a means for observing changes in temperature.
Possibilities: man's own reactions toward interpretation of temper-

---

[2] The teacher struggling with the problems of where one's definition of objectives leaves off and the teaching program begins is realizing—perhaps for the first time—that this is always a matter of judgment. Carried to the extreme, the teaching program is the final definition of the meaning of one's objectives. The task is to define the essential attributes to the point where the outlines of method, instruction, and evaluation are clearly worked out.

ature (degree) and changes (getting colder, hotter), thermometer (Farenheit, centigrade scales), wet bulb, electric.

Criteria of choice

A. How far to go in understanding heat, conduction, its action on cells, materials, man?

B. How far to go in understanding instrumentation?

III. *Need:* a means for observing and relating changes in temperature and their effect on man's living and for generalizing the basis of the results of observation.

A. Nature and range of observation:
1. for determining change.
2. for determining effect.

B. Procedures for interpreting and generalizing findings (scientific method).

This definition is obviously incomplete, but the essential three questions or operations involved in giving meaning to the objectives are indicated. If teachers have answers to these questions, the kind of evaluation form (e.g., multiple choice, essay, etc.) will be clearly indicated.

Definition in terms of behavior of children

The intent here is for the teacher to move from her direct consideration of her objectives to try to see what understanding of the objective would mean for the behavior of children. The reason for our insistence that a teacher needs to try to define her objective in terms of its essential components first is the feeling that most people cannot jump from the statement of the objective to the related behavior of the learner without this kind of analysis and help.

A common way to define this objective behaviorally is merely to list what individuals would do if they understood it (usually using some personal pronouns).

1. He can interpret what differences in temperature mean for what he wears when he goes to school.

2. He takes off his sweater when he plays a game and puts it back on when he is through.

3. He can read a Farenheit thermometer and record daily temperatures.

4. He can compare temperature at different times and determine temperature change.

5. He can translate temperature readings from a Farenheit scale to a centigrade scale.

6. He can predict the kinds of homes people will have by knowing the average temperature and its range over the year.

Enough is given here for the reader to realize what is being done and what it would mean for the process of definition. The relationship between this definition and the development of related appraisal devices should be reasonably clear.

Many teachers tend to confine their evaluations to the factual information covered and generally ignore the key area of abilities, social processes, and attitudes. Such objectives lend themselves especially to operational or behavioral definitions. Of course, many of these abilities and processes are now being evaluated only by actual observations of the child's behavior in appropriate situations.

Objective: To develop critical thinking.

Definition: 1. The perception of a problem situation involving more than one alternative.

2. Examination of range of identified alternatives.

3. Selection of reasonable hypothesis.

4. Determining of appropriate data or behavior to observe and record.

5. Determining and using appropriate methods of analysis and interpretation.

6. Drawing tentative conclusions and putting such generalizations into use for further evaluation.

The teacher can easily see how she could translate this definition into a behavioral one.

Another process objective: To develop ability to organize ideas in reading.

1. To recognize common elements in parallel topics or incidents or paragraphs.

2. To recognize proper time sequence.

Another objective: Skill in using a dictionary.
1. Spelling
2. Pronunciation
3. Syllabification
4. Plural forms
5. Parts of speech
6. Meaning

7

Organizing Centers

> *Perhaps the most crucial and central concept related to the teaching operations is the idea of the organizing center. As "the point where all the important aspects of the teaching act can be related and given focus," its effect on the quality of instruction can not be denied.*

> D. W. A.
> J. B. M.
> F. B. M.

It is difficult for anyone to have a very clear notion of the psychological unit of learning for another individual. This makes it necessary for the teacher to examine the nature of the centers of attention or interest around which he is attempting to organize the activities and behavior of children, and thus create some kind of unity of experience. Do these centers permit the child:

1. To relate his own sense of awareness and purpose to the center of attention being proposed?

2. To consider and evaluate the relationships which exist between him and the center of attention, educational goals, ideas, and procedures in effective learning?

3. To consider and evaluate the relationships which exist between one center and other foci of attention?

In any teaching situation the child is confronted by more than one thing to pay attention to and each topic permits development in many different directions. Thus there is no need to talk about "concomitant," "incidental," or "indirect" learning as another and different kind of learning. It is expected that any learning experience of sufficient comprehensiveness to include and hold the attention of a group of children will incorporate foci of attention on many different levels of importance, both to the child and to the educational goals being achieved.

Many of the problems of transfer of learning from one situation to another derive from lack of recognition by the teacher and children that familiar ideas and facts can be related to many different centers of attention. Transfer of learning is, therefore, aided when teachers help children perceive the relationships which exist between one focus of attention and another.

The topic, questions, problems, and objects which serve as centers of attention, besides providing a means for unifying experience, serve also as cues in learning. The past experience of the child is always the basis upon which he builds his future experience, and use of his past experience tends to reduce the time and effort involved in making a response to a center of attention. In this sense, the words in a reading lesson can only serve as a cue to the meaning that the child's past experiences have developed for him. This is the reason that some authors have defined readings as "bringing meaning to the printed page."

CONTINUITY OF LEARNING

Learning, particularly the purposeful learning of greatest importance to the school, always has a future—some extension in time, in logic, and in use. The continuity of his experience as seen by the child himself may not correspond to the sequential development of that experience as desired by the teacher or as indicated by the text or by other children. The teacher, if he is to be effective in promoting the development (continuity) of the child's learning, must become aware of what the child perceives as the extensions of his learning experiences.

The centers of attention perceived by children are the points at which the extensions in their learning take place. The problem is not whether or not there is continuity, but how to capitalize on the continuities that always exist in the ongoing experience of the child.

The continuity of a child's learning is strengthened if:

1. The instructional activities are organized around centers of attention which have valid extensions in understanding and in educational use.

2. There is constant effort to reach agreement among teacher, child, and other children about what they are trying to accomplish, and the relationships between that and other present and future activities to be developed.

3. The present planned sequences worked out in advance and provided for children—the next page, the next chapter, the simple-to-complex, the near-to-far, the immediate to the remote, the next topic to be covered, etc.—are tied into, and if possible grow out of, the actual perceived continuities in the child's learning experiences.

4. Skill programs, drill activities, etc. are developed in situations where applications are made and relationships are seen by the child as having some significance and educational perspective.

5. A constant, consistent effort is made to use the child's present and past experience as a basis for next steps, for moving to the next topic, for relating new centers of attention, and for evaluating the possible consequence of future plans.

QUALITIES OF GOOD ORGANIZING CENTERS

To be instructionally useful, organizing centers should have the following characteristics for teachers and children.[1]

1. *Qualities of significance.* For teachers, this means that the organizing center holds promise for developing in children those behaviors which come from deepening and broadening certain

---

[1] Virgil E. Herrick, "Approaches to Helping Children Improve Their Instructional Practices," *School Review*, LXII (December, 1954) pp. 533-34.

understandings, skills, and value referents that underlie the curriculum. For children, this means that the center holds promise for activities that are of intrinsic interest, and which they recognize as worthwhile.

2. *Qualities of accessibility.* More than geographic accessibility is implied here. Ideas, for example, must be made accessible to children in terms that they can understand. If the books expressing ideas which might be used as organizing centers even for young children are all written at the college level, then these ideas are lost as organizing centers. Accessibility in a physical sense means the proximity of nature trails, quarries, swamps, and other areas to serve as focal points for developing class activity.

3. *Qualities of breadth and scope.* If the entire class is to work as a single group, then the organizing center must lend itself to the demands of the many variations represented in that group. Similarly, the center must usually provide readily for moving several curricular elements along together, as well as a ready stimulant for writing, speaking, and speculating about significant life problems.

4. *Capacity for organizing and relating.* A likely organizing center is one that lends itself easily to learnings that have gone before and that are likely to lie ahead. It encourages children's efforts to "tie things together" and to perceive related wholes. Likewise, it facilitates the organization of group effort in such a way that individuals engage in worthwhile tasks with a minimum of time lost in getting started, accomplishing something, and moving ahead from task to task.

5. *Capacity for development.* A good organizing center encourages children to catch hold of it and then "to run with it." First explorations yield several alternatives for productive study. Action leads to new avenues that hold promise for further rich learning.

ILLUSTRATIVE ORGANIZING CENTERS

The deceptive and yet enchanting thing about the whole concept of organizing centers is that, instead of qualities such as those outlined above being inherent in a given center, the center is itself described, defined, and created by the qualities. In effect, the qualities are in the mind and eye of the viewer. The milkman kicks a pebble at the doorstep, and to him it is only a pebble. The geologist residing there picks it up and enchants his children for several nights with stories of how it came to be. The girl in the match factory watches the clock and thinks of the weekend ahead, while box after box passes under her scrutiny on the production line. The woodsman picks up a single match and brings forth endless tales of woodland giants, raging fires, and reforestation. To the geologist and the woodsman, a stone and a match are organizing centers for learning and teaching. An organizing center is whatever a teacher and a class can get their hands on and their minds around to enrich the quality of classroom living. Visualizing in the center the qualities that make it worthwhile determines the usefulness of that organizing center.

Since what is an organizing center for one teacher and class is not recognizable as such to another, the process of identification becomes complicated. Nonetheless, an attempt is made below to indicate some types of organizing centers for learning and teaching.

1. *Ideas.* Big ideas have traditionally served as organizing centers for learning: ideas about time, space, the future, man and his identity, the source of truth, and so on. Ideas, carefully selected, readily satisfy the requisites for good organizing centers for elementary school instruction. Ideas satisfy the criterion of development especially well; a group can take them and move with them. Problems of living are similar effective centers of attention for organizing learning.

2. *Materials.* On the assumption that teachers are guided more in setting up learning situations by the materials accessible to them than by any other single source of direction, most educators believe improvement of materials promises improvement of instruction. Teachers who depend heavily upon text materials, for example, are restricted by the suitability of these materials for the instructional goals they have in mind. If thinking about materials is extended to include encyclopedias, films, filmstrips, record players, and so on, it becomes obvious that materials hold much promise for classroom organization of instruction.

3. *Displays, Collections, Exhibits, etc.* To some, a science corner in the classroom is just a miscellaneous array of inanimate

or even animate "stuff." To others, it is a source of stimulating thought and activity. Book and science collections, museums, stamp and coin collections, and so on, offer much to the teacher who is able to see their possibilities for leading children into further exploration.

4. *Places.* Use of places as organizing centers ranges from playground application to foreign travel. Classes in Atlanta make effective use of places when they visit the Cyclorama to see the Battle for Atlanta brought to life in vivid color and form; in Pittsburgh groups go to the exact site of Fort Duquesne to study the past; in Detroit pupils visit an automobile factory to study mass production; in San Francisco they visit a cruiser in the Bay to compare naval equipment of past and present.

5. *People.* Much effective learning can be tied around names such as Columbus, Galileo, Disraeli, Handel, Shakespeare, Whitman, Franklin, and Ford.

In each instance given here, the idea, material, exhibit, place, or person represents a beginning point—an opportunity to get a toehold in profitable learning.[2] The intent to learn, however, becomes truly muddled when the vantage point, the organizing center, becomes a thing of inflated inherent value. Great names are important, yes; but the teacher who sees their potential for involving children in significant learning processes has a perspective that is fundamental to good teaching.

MULTIPLE AND INTERRELATED CAUSES

A persistent effort has been made in educational psychology to identify the individual stimulus connected with a particular response, in order that children's learning could be controlled and predicted. This has been accompanied by a similar attempt to analyze and subdivide educational goals into their simplest smallest components, so that children might master each one at a time and the particular stimulus-response pattern be identified and used

---

2 For a discussion of setting up a classroom to provide centers around which rich living can be organized, see Peggy Brogan and Lorene K. Fox, *Helping Children Learn* (New York: Harcourt, Brace & World, Inc., 1955) pp. 336–42.

to assure efficient learning. Psychologists forget, however, that the reacting agent in this effort is a very complex organism—the child; they also forget the breadth of experience each child brings to his learning in school, and the fact that he has a mind of his own. Who can determine the specific stimulus in the ordinary classroom situation which actuates the behavior of a particular child?

A teacher should not expect, then, that poor reading will be caused exclusively by poor vision; instead, he will try to examine those interacting factors which, because of their relationship to each other, offer a better explanation and prediction of learning than any single factor taken alone.

CENTERS OF ATTENTION SERVE AS ACTIVATORS OF BEHAVIOR

One concept of how to promote desirable learning involves trying to develop relatively automatic connections between the proper educational stimuli and the correct response. Then the presentation of the stimuli will activate the response desired. Many of the drill and mastery programs in the elementary school have been built on this kind of thinking about learning.

The concept that the center of attention or core of concentration in a learning experience may activate behavior does not discard what else is known about different aspects of learning; it merely focuses attention on what is significant in educational learning— the goal and its role in the control and direction of learning. In dealing with the accomplishment of an educational goal, be it learning how much is 3×4 or how we get our food, experience brings a reduction and differentiation in the behavior of a child in his attempts to deal with these goals. His behavior becomes more purposeful in the sense that he has discriminated among and re- duced the means necessary to accomplish what is desired. Future experience with these goals will allow the goal itself to activate behavior, not in the completely automatic sense, but in the sense of more thoughtful control and direction of behavior. This concept of learning is much more useful to the teacher than seeing learning as a series of simple stimulus-response patterns.

8

Evaluation

> *Evaluation is essential to all learning. It cannot be eliminated either from the learning process or the educational program of the school. It is just as essential a part of the teacher's growth as it is in promoting children's development.*
>
> *Virgil E. Herrick*

The importance of evaluation in education cannot be achieved either by denying it its place in educational development or by making it arbitrary, absolute, and penal in character. Neither is it accomplished by trying to find the "golden mean" of two poor practices or of a good and a poor practice. If there is any basis for judging "merit" in the educational behavior of children, this same basis should hold for judging merit in the instructional behavior of teachers.

WHAT IS EVALUATION?

Evaluation is a process which anyone carries on when he considers how well he is accomplishing what he set out to accomplish. In thinking about evaluation, two key ideas need to be kept clear: the concept of *a goal,* giving direction to the behavior being evaluated, and the concept of some *norm,* standard, or value being applied to the behavior to determine its adequacy. Evaluation is different from measurement in that measurement may determine that a table is seven feet long and four feet wide. Evaluation takes place when this table is considered from the point of view of a place to serve a meal to twenty people or only one, or examined to see if it will pass through a doorway two and a half feet wide and six and a half feet long, or considered as a place to work on a map five feet square or to store a thousand books. Measurement provides information for the evaluation process. Evaluation, however, goes on and places value on what measurement has found out. The words "appraisal," "assessment," and "testing" usually contain both of these ideas.

The root word in evaluation is *value.* In most cases, we as teachers or the children as learners are evaluating when we are judging the value of our activities to achieve our goals. This value judgment is of two parts; first, one judges whether what he is doing has something to do with his goal, be it arithmetic, history, or teaching (this is called *validity*), and second, one judges whether what he is doing in arithmetic, history, or teaching is adequate in relation to some known or imagined standard. There is a third judgment here, too; one we frequently overlook—namely, that the goal being worked on is worthy. Too often, other goals may be more important than the ones we are striving to achieve. We ought at least to consider this possibility.

THE ASPECTS OF THE
EVALUATION PROCESS

It is easy now to list the things that are necessary in all evaluation whether the teacher is evaluating the learning activities of Mary, John, or Susan in his class or whether the supervisor, principal, or a teacher is trying to evaluate the teaching activities of a given staff member. These things one must have:

You have to see what you are shooting at.

Some goal to achieve.

You have to try to achieve your goal.

Someone must be trying in some fashion to achieve that goal.

You have to look at what you have done.

Someone must observe that behavior.

You have to test the value of what you have done on the basis of some norm.

Some norm or standard is used to judge the adequacy of that behavior.

You have to arrive at some conclusion as to the value of your behavior.

Someone must make the judgment that (a) the observed behavior has to do with or is moving toward the accomplishment of the goal and (b) that the degree of accomplishment at this time is adequate.

You have to try to use the results of the evaluation to improve your future behavior.

Someone must attempt to put the results of the evaluation into practice. If the evaluations are to be educative, the behavior growing out of the evaluation should be more adequate than before.

This list of the necessary aspects of evaluation can be used by a child or teacher to check his present evaluation procedures in order to see if all the necessary steps are being considered or to identify points at which additional work needs to be done.

Most teachers and school faculties need to improve their evaluation programs at five major points:

1. Instructional goals should be stated and defined so that evaluations can be made of their accomplishment. Clearly perceived goals permit clear-cut evaluations.

2. The learning behavior of the child or teacher must be observed and recorded so that evaluations of that behavior can be made.

Our memories are notoriously short and we tend to see only what we want to see. Poor observations lead to poor and unreliable evaluations. Any test, be it objective or essay, is merely a standardized observation of the behavior of a child in specific situations with its own built-in recording system.

3. The norms or standards by which the adequacy of the goal behavior is judged must be clear.

Known, accessible, and developmental norms are just as important to adequate evaluation as are defined goals. Contrary to the usual expectation, a given goal and the behavior of a child may be judged on the basis of a number of different norms, thus providing a number of different judgments, all perfectly valid and necessary to the child's future development. The same is true of any teacher evaluation. The "value" of an evaluation is as good as its norm.

4. The judgments of value in the evaluation process must be used to improve the future behavior of the learner.

Evaluations should be educative and constructive and should not be penal and destructive. Too often the evaluation ends in terms of "A's," "75's," "3's," "upper 10 per cent'," or "inferior." Here the value is placed on the person and not on the knowledge, skill, or quality most useful in achieving a goal. Here, the consequence of the "A" is a pleasant feeling but, nevertheless, a dead end from the point of view of future behavior. It is the judge sentencing the person before the court; it is not the educational or developmental evaluation which values ways for improving learning or teaching or living.

5. The role of the learner (children, teachers, etc.) must be enhanced in the evaluation process.

It is possible to judge the behavior of a child or a teacher without the child's knowing that he is being observed, what goals are being checked, what norms are being applied, or what the final judgment is. Under these conditions it would be impossible for either the child or teacher to improve as a result of this kind of evaluation. Improvement of the learner comes as he is aware of the goals he is striving to achieve, what he has done, what norms are used, and what judgments are reached. Knowing these things, he can act intelligently to understand and improve his behavior.

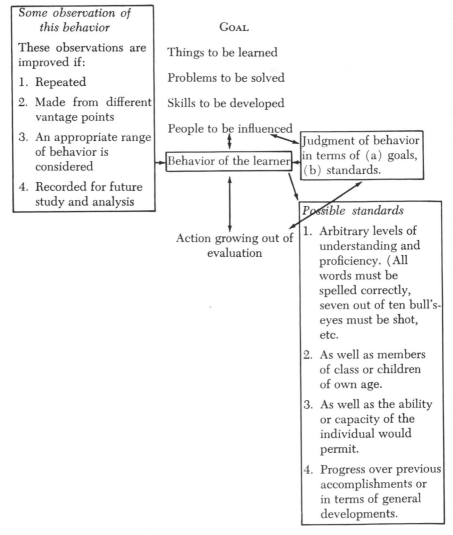

FIG. 6.   DIAGRAM OF THE EVALUATION PROCESS.

This diagram shows how the different aspects of the evaluation process are related and how some of those parts have been defined by various staffs.

THE ROLES PLAYED IN THE
EVALUATION PROCESS

It is helpful to look at evaluation from the point of view of the personal roles to be assumed in evaluation by the individuals involved. Frequently, these different roles to be played by people and their implications for the evaluation process are not seen. It is easy to forget that evaluation is always personal in reference, ultimately subjective in judgment, and individualized in consequence.

Four major roles which people can assume in the evaluation process can be identified as follows:

1. *The doer:* the child, teacher, or person whose behavior is being evaluated.

2. *The observer:* the person who is looking at what the learner is doing.

3. *The judger:* the person who is taking the results of the observations and judging their value and adequacy.

4. *The actor:* the individual who acts on the results of the evaluation.

One will soon recognize that these roles are not always played by different people. Commonly, for example, the child is the "doer" and the "actor," while the teacher is the "observer" and the "judger." If the evaluations are to become as educative as possible, then the child and the teacher have to make sure that the actors and doers work together with the observers and judgers. If the evaluation process is to become an integral part of the learning, then it is important that we study how the learner can have an important part in *playing all four roles.* This has important implications as to how the evaluation process can be developed with children and with school staffs. If evaluations of teachers and teaching are to be maximally educative, then the teacher must have an important part in or an understanding of the implications of these four roles in evaluation for his own development and understanding. Certainly, agreement among the various individuals involved in evaluation must be reached at two points—at the goals to be achieved and at the definition of the norms to be used.

DEFINING GOALS

One big stumbling block in evaluation is defining one's goal or objective. Most people agree that one can evaluate better if he knows clearly what his objectives are and has defined them in terms of the behavior which would characterize them. Then his observation of that behavior can be focused and valid. This may be illustrated by teachers working with children on a science unit on air. The teacher has identified six objectives she wishes to teach, i.e., the understandings and abilities she wishes children to gain as a result of this unit. They are as follows:

Understandings
  1. Air has weight.
  2. Air occupies space.
  3. Air exerts force.
  4. Air is a gas.

Abilities
  5. To gain skill in the experimental method:
     a. Identifying and defining a problem.
     b. Discovering the questions to ask.
     c. Developing ways to get answers to questions.
     d. Gathering, recording, analyzing appropriate data.
     e. Drawing conclusions.
     f. Acting on these conclusions.
  6. To gain skill in using materials and observation devices:
     a. Weather vane
     b. Anemometer
     c. Barometer

These objectives were related to what children did when they worked on the experiments, read the books and pamphlets, and applied their knowledge and skills. Consequently, the observational devices, the tests, rating sheets, check lists, and recordings could be planned and used by the children or teacher. All of this, however, was based on the careful definition of the objectives to be achieved.

Many times in practice, these objectives are not known in advance but grow out of the project or problem being worked on. In this case, the teachers and children are always generalizing and checking their generalizations as the ones they need to keep and use later. This same examination is made for the skills to be developed. In either case, however, whether the definitions of the objectives are made in advance or whether they grow out of the development of the project, the evaluation of the learning involved is based on this definition.

DETERMINING NORMS

Determining norms is perhaps the most difficult part of the evaluation process. Actually, it is much easier to define objectives, to develop observational devices, and to develop records for these observations than it is to decide upon the norm. The teacher, if he examines the norms indicated on the diagram, will see that as you move toward judging the child's behavior on the basis of his ability or on the basis of his relative progress, you are using the child as his own standard. Many feel that this is more educative than using some absolute standard or comparison with other groups of children or adults. At the same time, it should be recognized that all of these different norms answer different questions. The same behavior in arithmetic could be valued from the point of view of the child's going on to college and taking up engineering, in comparison with what others of his age are doing, in relation to his ability to learn arithmetic, and in relationship to the progress he has made during the past month. The use of these different norms provides additional meanings to the evaluation process.

The same observed behavior related to the same objective can be judged differently, depending upon the particular norm of adequacy that is applied.

Norm of the task itself

It is possible to identify some tasks which are sufficiently unitary to be completed on an all-or-none basis. With children a word is not spelled correctly until it is complete, a ball is not hit with a bat until the event actually happens, a step is not taken until it has occurred. With teachers, it is possible to say that a report is not handed in until it is received on the principal's desk or that discipline is not being maintained until all children are quiet when the teacher speaks. In this approach to adequacy, the task to be accomplished or essential aspects of the task are defined so as to include the conception of adequacy. The evaluation problem is merely to observe the behavior in such situations and to judge whether it is present or not.

Norm of the experience of others

In education most of our norms of behavior and achievement have been based on some measures of central tendency of a distribution of the accomplishments or judgments of an appropriate group of people.

Norm of the capacity of the individual

Another common position taken in determining adequacy is to judge the behavior as being adequate for a person in relation to his capacity to perform the task. Common measures of capacity in this sense are tests of mental maturity, appraisals of what is done now with what the individual has been able to do in the past, or estimates of the "task" potential or "ceiling" of the individual. These measures or estimates are used as a referent to compare present with past accomplishments and, on the basis of this norm, to judge them as to their adequacy.

Norm of what is socially or educationally desirable

Teachers, like all people, develop model patterns or expected behavior which they apply to the other teachers, the children, and the parents, and then make value judgments about these individuals on the basis of this conception. Whether this "model" is *right*, in the sense that it represents the most efficient pattern of behavior for accomplishing the work of a teacher or principal, is not the question.

The recognition of the role and function of this kind of norm in evaluating persons and activities in programs of in-service education is extremely important. Several suggestions as to ways to improve its use may be helpful.

1. Make the expectations of social and educational adequacy as explicit as possible in operational or behavioral terms. The question here is not whether this norm is used, but how it can be examined and consciously used to make evaluations constructive and educational. In many school staffs, it takes years for individuals to become aware of the codes of behavior that govern the status and success of people. These definitions can be made through the process of listing and organizing the behavior believed to be normative for a given professional or personal role. Similar procedures can be used for getting at how individuals perceive and value a particular problem or aspect of instructional practice.

2. Make comparisons among and between the various appropriate conceptions of actual and perceived normative behavior. This is of particular value in comparing methods and procedures of teaching—an area of behavior seldom examined by teachers and professional workers. One of the reasons for a lack of study in this portion of educational practice is that the normative basis for making valuing statements as to what is good is usually hidden and personal. Yet this area of activity represents a large portion of the time of most professional people. Evaluation procedures need to make it possible for the norm of social and educational expectancy to be recognized for the important role that it does play in our valuing of the many things we do and to get such definitions out in the open in order that they can be examined and constructively improved.

Norm of use

Generalizations are derived from present and past experience and then used to plan and direct future activities. If things get worse, the generalizing and/or the applications of that generalizing probably were not good. If things get better, then there is some confidence that these processes are of value and that the program is on the right track.

In the use of this norm, it should be recognized that generalizations as to ideas, processes, and values are intermingled. Other norms need to be applied as well in making final value judgments. The value of this norm of use is that it permits this kind of multiple evaluation to take place and that it provides an opportunity for any level of sophistication in evaluation to develop.

Norm of ends

Much of the previous discussion has to do with the evaluation of the goodness of means and the adequacy of development. It should also be recognized that the ends need to be appraised as to whether they are worth trying to achieve. The three common tests of ends have to do with their importance, their significance, and their cruciality.

The importance of an end is determined by its role and position in the program or field of knowledge that it represents.

THE DEVELOPMENT OF APPROPRIATE APPRAISAL DEVICES

This review up to this point suggests the following generalizations:

1. The key aspect of any evaluation program is the quality of the observations being made. One major tool for knowing you are looking at behavior which would enable you to draw worthwhile conclusions is to have these behaviors validated by carefully defined objectives.

2. Judgments of the adequacy of the behavior observed are determined by what norm is used. Different norms ask different questions of adequacy about the same behavior; any one or all of these norms might be important and necessary to any adequate planning for future learning behavior. This raises real questions about present marking and reporting systems. It suggests that a number of evaluations are necessary about any set of observations

and that no single grade or set of marks on a report card can communicate these evaluations. No evaluation is better than its norm.

3. The roles of individuals in the various phases of the evaluation process clarify what "self-evaluation" really means and define the kinds of communications among individuals in the evaluation process which are necessary if the evaluation is to be essentially educative for the learner (he sees better what to do next), not punitive.

4. It is possible to distinguish between the observations of an individual in a dynamic classroom situation and those in a structured test-item situation. In the test situation the behavorial response is limited and is usually categorized, unitized (can be counted), and scaled. In the classroom situation with broad limits for the actual response, the behavior usually is ongoing, complex, and interactive. It is hard to know what to count, how to categorize, and about the only scaling that is possible is to say, "It happens; these two behaviors are different, and this one is closer to our objective than the other." Yet this latter kind of evaluation situation forms the common fabric of the teacher's day and is probably more important to teaching and learning than the more formal test appraisal. We know a great deal more about test construction and use than classroom observation and evaluation. Perhaps we ought to do more about it.

5. The real concern in learning and teaching is whether changes are taking place in the behavior of the learner. Any single set of observations can say very little about change. Change can be determined only by the establishment of some benchmark against which to compare any given evaluation. This raises grave questions about the one-shot administration of achievement tests in the spring or fall of each academic year. We need to think more carefully about the evaluation of change and what this implies for evaluation in schools by teachers.

The last section of this chapter will attempt, therefore, to do three things: (1) to take our defined objective and build sample test items to point out the problems; (2) to examine the classroom situation where we are trying to evaluate the critical thinking, and finally (3) to draw some generalizations about the teacher and her role in the evaluation process.

SAMPLE TEST ITEMS

The common kinds of test items used by teachers have been the essay question and the so-called "objective" type of question: true-false, yes-no, multiple-choice, completion, and matching items. We are confining our illustrations to two kinds—the essay question and the multiple-choice items.

Essay question

The essay type of question provides opportunity for the student to interpret, relate, project, and organize his understanding of the topic being examined. It is less useful to deal with the factual aspects of the subject matter covered—other kinds of test items can do this better. In general, teachers should avoid using essay-type questions to cover the four W's of testing—who, what, where, when.

Objective: Differences in temperature affect the way man lives.

Sample essay questions:

1. You hear over the radio at breakfast that the low and high temperatures predicted for the day will be 25° F and 50° F, with snow in the morning turning to rain in the afternoon.
   a. What difference would this information make to you in your going to school?
   b. What difference would this information make to a man driving to work?
   c. What difference would this information make to the man in charge of streets?

2. You are making a thermometer. How would you determine the scale for measuring temperature?

Even these two examples begin to reveal some of the problems of an essay question. The difficulties of setting up the situation to which the student must respond, how further to structure or direct the nature and range of the responses, and how to make sure that every aspect of the question is equally meaningful to each test taker are problems of concern to every teacher.

It is obvious, too, that one essay question alone is not able to adequately cover the scope of the objective being tested. Putting on a raincoat and rubbers to go out to school covers only one aspect of man's living. The total test must have adequate coverage. One helpful way to check this is to key each essay question to each objective or aspect of it.

A third factor is clear. The writing of the test question— not the objective—forces the teacher to adjust her test item to the age, background, and ability of her children. The above questions, for example, could not be used with primary children.

A fourth problem is apparent when such questions are administered to students. What is an adequate answer to any question which stresses thought, interpretation, depth of understanding? One way to test an essay question is to try to answer it and consciously to explore the range of possible acceptable answers.

A fifth question grows out of the former problem. How are you going to value any particular answer? What is the value of an individual test question in the whole text? How do you quantify the scoring of an essay question?

A final problem of an essay exam is the difficulty in using such exams to evaluate change over time in the learning of students. The difficulty of establishing a common base for determining change is apparent.

Multiple choice items

Bloom and others [1] have given us perhaps the most useful set of categories for dealing with knowledge, comprehension, application, analysis, synthesis, and evaluation in the development of test items. It is not possible to demonstrate these different kinds and levels of understanding with test items related to an objective. One or two may suffice to indicate what might be done.

---

[1] Benjamin S. Bloom, ed., *Taxonomy of Education Objectives: The Classification of Education Goals*, Handbook I; Cognitive Domain (New York: David McKay Co., Inc., 1956) p. 207.

Knowledge of Specifics

1. Temperature is measured by:
———a. A barometer
———b. A thermometer
———c. A clinometer
———d. A pedometer
———e. A speedometer

Comprehension

2. A magazine article said that an unprotected man on the moon would freeze to death at night and burn to death during the day. This would happen on earth as well if:
———a. The blanket of air were stripped away from the earth.
———b. The sun were closer to the earth.
———c. The earth did not spin on its axis.
———d. We did not wear clothes to protect us.

These two examples show that the different possible responses in a test item must appear equally plausible and that the understanding of the student must make the difference in his answer, not his general intelligence or capacity to guess.

EVALUATION OF CRITICAL THINKING
IN CLASSROOM SITUATIONS

Very few tests have been constructed to measure critical thinking, yet few lists of objectives omit this important skill. As has been pointed out, most of the evaluations of thinking processes grow out of the broad range of observations teachers make of individuals in problem-solving situations in classrooms, in laboratories, on the playground, and in the wide scope of things which constitute the life of students in school. Although it would be impossible to cover this problem adequately in this paper, it is possible to point out what has to be done.

1. The definition of critical thinking in terms of its operations provides the initial basis for thinking through the kind of behavior

to be observed. Time spent by teachers in thinking this and the following step through will pay great dividends later. Here, each aspect of critical thinking can be further subdivided into specific behaviors.

a. Most teachers will find that it is important to utilize the work of other people in this process of finding the most significant aspects of critical thinking to observe. Works by B. S. Bloom and Lois Broder,[2] and Robert L. Thorndike [3] should be helpful; David Russell's recent book, *Children's Thinking*, is perhaps most useful of all. The idea is to find the fewest aspects of behavior which would determine the nature and amount of critical thinking of any one individual. Or, to say this differently, the observations should permit one to distinguish between individuals in respect to the character and degree of their critical thinking.

b. Many teachers might want to approach this problem by going directly to the observation of children working in problem-solving situations. Anecdotal records kept consistently on one child over a period of time as he works in many different kinds of critical-thinking situations would provide valuable materials for group study. Teachers might find that our classical statements of the thinking process do not exist in the same way in the thinking behavior of people. In addition, these records would provide a case book on the actual behavior of children in thinking situations. This material should prove extremely valuable in developing observation forms, rating scales, and the like.

A second way to get at this task is to observe a child working on a problem and then to discuss with him what he did in thinking through his solution. Those interviews are always improved if you work out a schedule of things to investigate with each child.

2. A second problem is how to cut down one's evaluation task to workable size. The staff may want to restrict their study to thinking in only one area—in science, in arithmetic, or in social

---

[2] Bloom and Broder, *Problem Solving Processes of College Students*, a supplementary educational monograph (Chicago: University of Chicago Press, 1950).

[3] Thorndike, "How Children Learn the Principles and Techniques of Problem Solving," Chap. 8 in Forty-Ninth Yearbook, Part I of the National Society for Study of Education (Learning and Instruction) (Chicago: University of Chicago Press, 1950) pp. 192–216.

situations, etc. Frequently this helps get the work of the evaluation within what teachers feel they can do.

3. The next step is building the observation device, check sheet, or rating scale for use in directing and recording observations. Many teachers feel they can observe and record actual behavior; they feel less comfortable in making judgments about frequency or value at the same time. We suggest that this should be done later. Other decisions have to do with how many children to observe, how often, in what situations, and for how long.

4. A further step deals with the problem of what to do with these records of observations after you have made them. Here the problem of counting and categorizing comes into focus. One way would be to count each instance of behavior and list it under the appropriate heading. This permits some diagnosis of the thinking act. A common way is to lump together all instances of thinking behavior and get a group score. In doing this, some teachers have judged "identifying a problem" and "determining key questions" as being more important than "collecting data." A rough series of weights for each kind of thinking behavior could be assigned according to judgment of relative value.

5. These gross scores can be examined at this point in a number of ways: (1) A distribution of such individual scores can be made and individuals can be examined as to their relative placement (Observation techniques are hard to apply to total class or age group or to use in observing every individual in a group.) (2) The record of these observations can be kept and discussed as a basis for comparing future observations of the same individual and for making analyses of changes (in the thinking act). If this is done, it will be desirable to make some examination of what constitutes development in thinking. Gross frequency scores may not be enough. One may wish, too, to try to develop a model of critical thinking and to judge growth as progress towards this model. In this last approach the comparison is in respect to the behavior of one individual; therefore, the problems of background, level of intelligence, and degree of opportunity do not bear on the observation process—only on the interpretation and prediction phases.

6. The problem of how to develop norms, models, and records as a means for studying and interpreting changes over time is a

fundamental problem seldom faced realistically in many schools. This phase of evaluation alone needs considerable exploration.

7. Every staff group, as they move into evaluations based on direct observations, need expert help and encouragement. This point has implications for the kind of consultant help to secure for staff work or for the personnel to be added to the central office.

GENERAL CONCLUSIONS

Obviously, many problems have been left unexplored, but we hope enough has been said to indicate a number of important areas for significant work:

1. We need to go back to objectives and consider their derivation, statement, and definition problems as a fundamental background for all evaluation attempts. Improvement here will automatically improve our evaluation.

2. We can do a great deal to improve our knowledge of the part the observation process plays in evaluation and of ways to improve its procedures.

3. If the role of the individual learner is important in evaluation, then the present examination of the key roles in the evaluation process will help us see what self-evaluation means and what educational evaluation really involves.

4. A key problem, greatly ignored, is the one of determining appropriate norms or standards for judging adequacy. We have tried to indicate the range of norms necessary properly to interpret and appraise educational behavior, but this problem needs further study for it has great implications for the problem of grading, reporting, and parent-teacher-child conferences.

5. The general area of abilities and attitudes lacks appropriate appraisal devices and procedures. Most of our evaluation devices have to do with the appraising of subject matter and of intellectual power. We need to develop better evaluations in the area of abilities in language, thinking, social processes, and in the use of learning resources. Observations by teachers and students offer a promising way of starting evaluations in the important areas of the educational program.

6. Contrary to general belief, we feel that the usual achievement tests found in national survey batteries used at the elementary school level in the areas of language arts, social studies, science, and health are not very adequate. Any school staff with no more than usual resources could build achievement examinations which are many times more valid, more reliable, and just as well constructed. In addition, diagnoses and interpretations growing out of the use of such tests would have real meaning for better teaching and learning in a given school system.

7. The only educational justification for evaluation is that it leads to more effective learning and teaching. Unless the results of evaluations are plowed back into student and teaching behavior, the time and effort which have gone into this enterprise cannot be justified. This point of view has real implications for those who are to be involved in evaluation, the kind of communications which should exist, and the nature of the administrative procedures which are necessary to achieve this goal. The finest of evaluation devices cannot rise any higher than their use.

9

Curriculum Decisions And Provisions For Individual Differences

> *It is the thesis of this chapter that all of classes of decision-making are important and related; no one category can be omitted from adequate educational planning for individual differences. Further, decisions about matters which deal with goals and instructional strategies to accomplish them, and those which deal with individuals and with human dignity and respect, have first priority; they should precede and control rather than follow decisions where administrative arrangements for children, teachers, time, space, and materials are dominant considerations.*
>
> **Virgil E. Herrick**

A teacher makes a number of different kinds of educational decisions when dealing with the problem of individual differences within his classroom. One type of decision has to do with the selection of objectives, the topic being studied, the organizing center being used, the instructional plan considered appropriate, and the nature of the evaluation desired. A second class of decisions has to do with how individual children are recognized and respected, how teacher and pupil roles are determined, and how the interpersonal dynamics of the classroom are directed to more adequate personal, social, and educational ends. A third class of decisions has to do with the way children and teachers are grouped, the way time and space are used, and the way instructional materials and resources are obtained and related. Every teacher has to deal with all three of these classes of decisions. Most, if not all, of the provisions for dealing with individual differences in the classroom fall within these categories.

Too often we start with an administrative commitment to a teaching machine, to a teaching team and a group of ninety children (or for that matter, to a group of twenty-five children), and then we consider what directives these decisions have for instruction, rather than vice versa.

This thesis can be documented by examining briefly two of the decisions in the first category which confront every teacher every day that he teaches. These two decisions have to do with determining the nature and the level of the teacher's instructional objectives and the nature and the characteristics of the organizing centers which he selects for teaching and learning.

Several other decisions in curriculum could have been used for this discussion. The nature and the priorities of the screens for selecting learning activities and the nature and roles of the teacher and learner in the evaluation process in instruction would have served equally well. The conclusion growing out of the two areas selected will illustrate the point being made.

A LOOK AT INSTRUCTIONAL OBJECTIVES IN RELATION TO INDIVIDUAL DIFFERENCES

One of our most ancient and most persistent notions about the teaching-learning act is that it ought to be purposeful—goal-centered—and directed by significant educational objectives. Few disagree with this general proposition. If this conception of the teaching-learning act is sound, a careful study of these objectives, their nature, and their use in making educational decisions should furnish many suggestions for providing for individual differences. An examination of how teachers use objectives would suggest several conclusions about how many teachers perceive objectives in their instructional practices.

1. Many teachers do not understand the difference between objectives and organizing centers. For example, teachers state their objective as "To teach Chicago" rather than seeing understandings like, "Man works with other men to meet their common needs" as the objective and Chicago as a representative city which can be used to achieve some appreciation of this generalization.

Thus the phrases "to educate children," "to teach Chicago," or "to develop an understanding of the simple sentence" are not objectives. The first is a generality that states the total task of the school. The second is a possible organizing center to be used to develop certain understandings or objectives. The third avoids the issue by not stating what a simple sentence is.

A teacher's statement of instructional objectives is more useful in making curriculum decisions if this statement does not include principles of learning, important organizing centers, a list of instructional materials, propositions about the good life, and the kitchen sink.

If a teacher can distinguish between important understandings and intellectual processes as objectives and the other necessary components of curriculum, he is freer to think imaginatively about the many different topics, areas, objects, and centers of interest which can be used to provide for the individual differences of children and yet deal with the important understandings and thought processes of the educational program.

In providing for individual differences in the classroom, teachers must realize that in any comprehensive teaching act, several important curriculum decisions have to be made. Determining your instructional objectives is only one of these decisions. Equally important is the realization that objectives can perform certain curriculum functions and that they cannot perform others. Failure to make these distinctions creates real obstacles to providing adequately for the individual differences of children.

2. Many teachers fail to distinguish between objectives seen as facts and speicfic skills, and objectives seen as major concepts of the subject area, and key intellectual and social processes.

How a teacher sees and defines his instructional objectives plays an important part in determining how he will provide for the individual differences of children.

Stenographic records of classroom episodes taken from schools in "Prairie City," a typical midwestern community studied by the Human Development Committee of the University of Chicago and from schools in Texas, Michigan, Illinois, and Wisconsin communities, were used to examine how teachers perform their many instructional tasks. Our analysis of these records shows three important findings.

First, many teachers see their content objectives at the level of the specific fact and thus deal with objectives such as "Robins have red breasts," "five fours are twenty," "the letter h is formed with a straight line and a half loop," and "Chicago is on Lake Michigan."

When a teacher sees his instructional objectives in this way, adaptations for individual differences are forced in certain directions. The teacher may vary the speed with which children move through these particulars. The teacher may make adaptations in instructional materials—workbooks, drill exercises, flash cards—so that the child can work on those things which he does not know. The teacher may devise grouping procedures which will bring together children who are at approximately the same place in the hierarchy of things to know and to verbalize.

Some teachers view their objectives, however, as broader in scope and strive to teach such concepts as "a number may express either the idea of how many or the idea of relationship," or "the area of any rectangular surface is dependent upon the length of its base and height," or "man influences and is influenced by his environment."

When a teacher sees his instructional objectives as teaching concepts, his classroom provisions for individual differences tend to use a wider variety of related activities and experiences to help children deal with understandings on many levels of conceptualization and in respect to many different sets of particulars. The teacher tends to see no single learning experience as having a one-to-one relationship to the mastery of these concepts. The way is opened for many possible adaptations to be made in the learning experiences of children. If the teacher does not see how he can achieve his objectives through many possible instructional means, the only alternatives open to him for variation in his teaching are children, time, and materials.

With this latter perception of objectives, teachers are more likely to see broader objectives as having meaning for both the kindergarten child and the high school senior. They do not spend time in curriculum committees trying to define the level of understanding to be reached by first-, fourth-, or sixth-grade children. This important fact is always being defined by the children themselves. Thus, the child himself becomes an important agent in determining many of the necessary provisions for his own learning. Actually, he is the only one who has much of the necessary information.

Second, many teachers who see their instructional objectives at the level of the fact tend to organize their instruction around these specifics directly and use instructional procedures that stress recognition, verbalism, and memory. Thus, this kind of teacher sees no problem in teaching "Three fours are twelve" as "Three fours are twelve" or "Air has weight" as the verbalism "Air has weight." His objective, therefore, becomes the unit of instruction to be taught directly. Our analysis indicates that when a teacher sees his instructional objectives as learning specifics, this perception limits the possible ways in which he can provide for pupils' individual differences.

Third, many teachers who see their instructional objectives at the level of the fact tend to ignore the importance of the whole array of skills—language skills, thinking skills, social skills, and skills in the use of instructional materials—which are regarded as important instructional objectives in every curriculum program.

Again, our data seem to indicate that when a teacher sees process objectives as being a necessary part of any classroom activity, he tends to organize his classroom instruction around organizing centers which properly include these skills. His organizing centers thus tend to be more comprehensive and provide more opportunity for the use of various levels of skill, for many different vehicles for skill development, and for many more appropriate areas of skill application—all important conditions which would make possible desirable instructional provisions for individual differences.

ORGANIZING CENTERS AS FACTORS IN DETERMINING PROVISIONS FOR INDIVIDUAL DIFFERENCES

In our examination of learning episodes, the importance of the role of the organizing center in the instructional process soon became apparent. The more we thought about objectives and their nature and directives for instruction, the more we realized that if instructional objectives are important understandings and learning processes, then you did not teach them directly, but you had to select some vehicle or vehicles to provide the means for their accomplishment.

These vehicles—the questions the teacher asked, the example or problem posed, the objects to be examined, and the zoo to be visited and observed—all formed organizing centers to which the children and teacher related their activities and to which they applied their thinking, generalizing, and personal action.

An organizing center for instructional purposes is any object, idea, person, question, or instructional material used to relate and focus the thinking and action of an individual or a group. Organizing centers can be defined better by their organizing functions than by their nature.

A picture is not an organizing center for instruction because it is a picture. Rather, it is an organizing center because the eyes and thoughts of a class of children focus on it and their learning behavior is related to it in some kind of active fashion.

If a picture is not the object of attention and educational action by some individual or group, it is not an organizing center. An object becomes an organizing center only when it becomes the focus for such action by these individuals. The nature of a center does not of itself make it a center; its nature merely permits and enhances such focusing and organizing behavior.

Nerbovig[1] in her study found that teachers talked about teaching addition, the farm, electricity, and the seven basic foods as their

---

[1] Nerborvig, *Teachers' Perception of the Functions of Objectives,* unpublished Ph.D. thesis (Madison, Wisconsin: University of Wisconsin, 1956).

objectives rather than identifying the understanding and the processes commonly assumed to be objectives.

To us this finding indicated that many teachers start their educational planning with their organizing centers rather than with their objectives. Actually, this is a much more realistic and useful curriculum decision in their eyes than the decision that "a simple sentence is a single complete unit of thought."

These analyses forced the author to hypothesize that if an organizing center is to make it possible to meet the individual needs of the children who participate in its development, it should have the following characteristics.

1. *More than one dimension of accessibility.*

If an organizing center can be attacked in more than one way by the learner, its power to provide for individual differences is increased.

If a teacher poses a question as a center for thought and action and presents the question orally, he limits its accessibility. If he asks the question orally and also writes it on the chalkboard, he increases the accessibility of the question for learning. None of the child's energy has to go into remembering the question, so if the question has any significance for him, he is freer to concentrate his full attention on its study and resolution.

Even though the teacher speaks and writes the question on the board, if the necessary information to deal with it is provided only by the teacher, he limits its accessibility to children. If, however, the necessary information to deal adequately with the question can be acquired by children through observation, manipulation, reading, and other sources for knowing, the accessibility of the organizing center to children for learning is correspondingly increased.

If the question is such that responses to it are limited to one word, to "yes" or "no" responses, its capacity to deal with individual differences is more limited than if this were not true.

If the map on the board is large enough for all to see and is placed properly, its accessibility to more than one child is increased. If the map is too small or is poorly placed, its accessibility for learning is decreased. Or, if work is to be done on the map, the map is more accessible to children if each child can have a copy.

An organizing center is more accessible to more than one child if it properly involves the participation of two or more individuals. Sending a note to the principal does not need the five children we sometimes send with it. One child can run this errand, although we may justify this action by claiming that the other four are getting better acquainted with their school environment. Organizing centers that consist of spelling words, vocabulary words in reading, or combinations in arithmetic seldom involve more than one child and thus permit only certain limited adjustments to individual differences.

All that has been said may seem elementary, but it has become obvious to the author that it does not matter how we manipulate the variables of ability and accomplishment, the number of individuals involved, the pacing of the learning process, and the materials and physical space. Unless the organizing center for the learning is accessible to the children, no real provision for individual differences can be made.

2. *More than one level of accomplishment.*

If an organizing center is to have the capacity to provide for individual differences, it must have a low catch-hold points and high ceilings. An earthworm can provide a challenge to a kindergarten child and to a college senior; to a child with limited experience and limited capaci.y to learn, as well as to a child with rich experience and gifted capacities. This principle applies to organizing centers like the common and persistent problems of living in social studies, creative writing in language arts, and learning more about our weather in science.

Many teachers, however, use organizing centers which have narrow limits for knowing and learning, such centers as spelling the word *cat*, locating the capital of Illinois, naming the parts of speech, or working examples in arithmetic. Each of these centers limits the child to one level of accomplishment. Each provides little opportunity for individual differences. A teacher's alternatives are to slide a child up and down these specific centers until he finds one the child can do, or he spends enough time on one until the child finally grasps the proper response.

3. *More than one dimension of mobility.*

One of the most important problems in curriculum planning is the one of knowing how to insure proper continuity in a child's learning. Everyone wants one lesson in reading to contribute to the next one. Every teacher wants to help every child transfer his knowledge of his own community to his attempts to understand the lives of people more remote in space and time.

It seems clear that if a teacher can select organizing centers which have the capacity to move in time, in space, in cultures, and in logic, these centers have greater capacity to provide for individual differences than when this is not true.

In social studies, for example, such centers as great people, great documents, cities, states, or countries are commonly used as organizing centers, but they have limited mobility. It is hard to move Madison, Wisconsin anywhere else. But social functions, common geographic characteristics or the common and persistent problems of living, all have the capacity to move in time, in space, in cultures, and in logic. They have greater capacity, therefore, for providing room and opportunity for encompassing meaningfully, differences in children's background, ability, and development than centers which lack this capacity.

If we checked proposed organizing centers in social studies programs against this criterion, we would go a long way toward providing a more effective instructional base for dealing with individual differences in this field. Unless instruction is organized around centers which provide room for individuals to vary and to zoom in understanding as far as they can go, few effective instructional provisions can be made for individual differences.

4. *More than one degree of organizing capacity.*

Some teachers favor a main organizing center that has several important subcenters that have to be studied if the children are to get a proper understanding of the whole. The *home* is one good example. As children study the home, subcenters such as the responsibilities of children and parents in the home, how such problems as food, clothing, earning money, and recreation are handled, how the different rooms of the house are used, and how the house is placed in a community of houses—all provide a means for individual and/or small group study and exploration. Yet all these enterprises are seen as important and relevant parts of the main area of concern. It is felt that this kind of organizing center gives many more opportunities for providing for individual differences than one like *"pets."* Yet *"pets"* provides greater organizing scope than naming locations, describing objects, and drawing up lists—centers commonly used by many teachers.

This examination of how decisions in two common areas of curriculum planning can contribute to more adequate provisions for individual differences suggests the following conclusions:

1. The decisions the teacher makes about the important components of curriculum direct and limit the nature of the provisions that can be made for dealing with individual differences.

2. Teachers who see their instructional objectives at the level of factual specifics tend to provide for individual differences through variations in time, in amount to be learned, in numbers of children, and in instructional materials. The things to be learned tend to remain constant at the specific level for all children.

3. Teachers who see their instructional objectives at the level of important generalizations and key intellectual and social processes are more willing to explore a wider variety of means for accomplishing those objectives and are more willing to accept a wider range of levels of understanding and accomplishment.

4. The capacity of a learning center to provide for individual differences depends on the extent to which such centers meet the following criteria. They need to have more than one dimension of accessibility, more than one aspect of mobility, and more than a single degree of organizing capacity.

When these conditions are met, the teacher has an organizing base for instructional activities which will include more than one child, will provide room for many levels of contribution, will permit children to move in many important directions, and will help them explore an adequate number of important relationships. The provision of this kind of instructional base lies close to the heart of our problem of providing adequately for the individual differences of children.

10

Achieving Social Goals

Every teacher who works with young children is frequently perplexed by the problem of how to select and organize their learning experiences in order to achieve social goals.

This chapter can be of greatest value to the teacher by showing the tools and curriculum processes through which the teacher may select experiences and, through them, help the children achieve desirable social ends. The tools are four in number: (1) the objectives for social studies instruction; (2) the plan of sequence for the social studies program; (3) children's interests; and (4) instructional resources. The importance given to each of these factors will differ according to the way in which the curriculum is organized.

Virgil E. Herrick

DEFINITION OF OBJECTIVES

Social studies objectives are stated in a variety of ways. Each has advantages and limitations which will help the teacher determine which experiences are most appropriate for his class.

Objectives stated as *social* or *geographic areas* take such form as: "to help children adjust to school life," or "to help children learn about Holland." They tell the teacher very directly what broad topics or areas must be taught, but provide no clue as to which of many possible experiences should be included in each area.

Objectives stated as *concepts* give the teacher more flexibility. He can narrow the scope of what is to be taught and at the same time expand his choice of topics. Take, for example, these two statements: "Many people contribute to school life," and "To help children adjust to school life." The first, stated as a concept, gives the teacher a more precise definition of what should be taught than the second, which merely indicates a social area.

On the other hand, if the teacher restates the objective "To learn about Holland" in the form of a concept, such as "People can modify their natural environment," he can expand his choice of topics to other areas than Holland—the Mississippi levees, for instance, or even a local flood-control project.

It is important to note, however, that objectives stated as concepts will not tell the teacher which topic is most appropriate.

Instructional objectives are stated in terms of *social processes* or *social problems,* such as "producing," "conserving," "transporting," and "governing." Unlike the two previous approaches, the teacher does not assume sole responsibility for determining what will be taught, but participates with children in identifying their problems in these areas. In answering such questions as "How do we get our food?" or "What does our community do to protect our health?" decisions have to be made as to how deeply children will probe into the problems as well as how broadly they will view them. Objectives in themselves will not tell the teacher how detailed the answers (learning experiences) should be.

The emerging needs or problems of children can be used as a means for determining the educational objectives. Problems such as "How can I keep from catching a cold?" or "What is the safest route for me to take to school?" indicate quite clearly the nature of the learning experiences which must take place in order that children's needs or concerns be met. They suggest, too, that the range or breadth of experiences selected to meet these needs will depend upon the way in which children live and function *now,* rather than as adults. What they don't tell the teacher is which of an endless list of children's needs are properly the concern of the school.

In addition to the above four types of objectives dealing with ideas or content of various subject fields, there are accompanying objectives centering on the ways in which children work in using subject matter. These processes include such things as study skills, communication, and human relationships. Hence, the teacher must select experiences from the standpoint of both content and processes. He must ask himself two questions: "What learning experiences will best convey the appropriate ideas to children?" and "Which of these is best suited for promoting the next steps in the continuous improvement of working or processing objectives?"

WHAT IS SEQUENCE PLANNING?

Sequence plans attempt to establish continuity of learning experiences throughout the social studies program.

A plan based on *holidays and events* of the year or of topics to be covered can be approached quite directly by the teacher. In addition to asking himself what experiences develop the concept and solve the problem, he must also determine which ones are in keeping with the calendar. This is one way of bringing about an integration of school experiences with activities outside. Holidays, however, seem to have "just happened," and do not provide for the logical development of learning experiences.

A familiar pattern of social studies sequence is based on *geographic areas* and progresses from home to school, to community, to state, and so on. This, too, can be used quite directly by the teacher. In addition to identifying experiences which might serve to cultivate a safety consciousness, for example, the teacher must select those which apply to the particular geographic area assigned to her grade. A first-grade teacher will thus be concerned with safety experiences in the home and school, whereas the focus of the third grade might be on community safety. Although this plan is supported in part by research, which indicates a gradual expansion of children's horizons from the immediate to the remote, progression is not as uniform or fixed as the plan would seem to indicate. Children do not live for a whole school year in a single geographic area.

A third way of planning for sequence is in terms of *expanding areas of social experience*. This is the most common definition used in the primary grades. One illustration is the familiar expanding circle: home, school, neighborhood, community, region, hemisphere, and world. Another is to use the common problems of social living as themes whereby one can move with children to other geographic areas and time periods. The big problem here is how to use this definition of sequence so as to help a pupil understand a world which may be beyond his immediate community at nine years, and then how to keep his immediate community tied into the world which he covers at such a furious pace at twelve.

Of course, every teacher of young children will recognize that he has at some time or other used all of these plans. The important point here is that the definition of sequence, added to that of social goals, gives the teacher a two-way referent for selecting the experiences children should have. The sequence definition says that you consider the home and school in the first grade, and the goals definition indicates the kinds of learnings to be achieved through the study of the home and school.

CHILDREN AND TEACHING RESOURCES

Two other major tools for selecting and developing experiences are the children's interests and the instructional materials and resources found in the school and community. Social goals can be achieved through many kinds of experiences. Those centered in the social concerns of children provide a powerful tool for education. A teacher will want, therefore, to observe and plan with her pupils. Every teacher knows, however, that many interesting experiences fail to materialize because of lack of proper materials or the opportunity to make a trip. The most effective learning experience is one that brings children and instructional resources together in achieving social goals.

THE ORGANIZING CENTER

One of the most important curriculum decisions a teacher makes is the selection of an organizing center for focusing and relating the activities, ideas, and attention of a group of young and lively children.

If intended as a focus, any question, map, picture, or promenade should provide some chance of achieving social goals, fitting into the sequence definition, and utilizing interests and resources. This is a matter of first consideration. There are, however, other characteristics of good organizing centers which will help a teacher recognize them as they come along or as he dreams them up.

Is the organizing center physically and intellectually accessible to children?

If a teacher asks a question children cannot hear, shows a map they cannot see, or proposes an activity in which they cannot engage, it is not likely that these centers are accessible to children for thought and action. Nor are they accessible if so far removed from children's experience that their meaning can only be surmised. An organizing center is a good vehicle for achieving social goals if children can get their "sense" fingers into it and tie it in with what they are doing—that is, if they can read, talk, hear about it, and work on it. Social goals will not be achieved by children if they cannot catch hold of the experiences which will effect their realization.

Does the organizing center have adequate comprehensiveness?

If 25 children are involved, does the center under consideration have sufficient intellectual and operational breadth to include the looking, thinking, and acting of that number? Taking a note to the principal should not require 25 children; planning and putting on a tea for the mothers should not be the responsibility of one child. The best organizing centers are comprehensive enough to include children, a number of subcenters, a variety of activities, multiple tools for learning, and some opportunity for responsible action and testing of understandings and values. Many of our social goals are concerned with effective language use, constructive critical thinking, the arts of living and working together, and responsible, thoughtful, social action. It is, therefore, especially important that any organizing center should encourage the development of these goals in terms which make them significant and meaningful to children. An organizing center, to be a good one in this sense, must have sufficient scope to permit these social and intellectual processes to be developed. Listing the capital of the state, the mayor of the town, and representatives in Congress would not provide this kind of opportunity. Seeing how the firemen at the local fire house serve us might.

Does the organizing center have the capacity for going anywhere?

From the point of view of achieving social goals, this is a most important characteristic. A good organizing center must have the capacity for intellectual and social movement. It should permit ideas, people, and social and cultural behavior and values to move from place to place and from one time to another. For this reason, questions which have limited, factual answers are not good organizing centers. Similarly, people, geographic places, and objects are not good long-term organizing centers for achieving social goals. It is hard to go anywhere with them. How does one move Madison, Wisconsin, anywhere else? It is unique. What does one do in Fall River, Massachusetts, with Chicago's famous people? Common problems of living and social action are much better, because they permit movement backward and forward in time, cultural extensions to many people and places, and intellectual examination of the ideas and processes which people have used to deal with these problems. A good organizing center must have staying power, so that children can examine it over a period of time; it must also permit personal, geographic, time, and cultural extensions in order that children can constantly broaden and enrich their understanding of themselves and of their social world.

Organizing centers, then, should be accessible, comprehensive, and movable.

The story which follows of a quarrel over space on the school ground shows how some of the ideas discussed in this chapter have been put into practice.

EPISODE: PEER GROUP PROBLEMS

One afternoon Peter and Joe walked into their classroom towards the middle of the recess period, trying to look unconcerned and innocent. "What are you doing inside?" their teacher asked. "We were sent in. We were chasing the girls," was their reply. After talking the incident over with the teacher, they said they could take care of themselves, and the day passed as usual. Next morning, when the recess bell rang, they came directly to their teacher with this information: "We chased the girls again—honest, we tried not to, but they heckled us so that we just had to." By this time the girls had arrived to defend their position.

As they talked, the problem finally was defined. It seemed there was a choice spot on the playground where both wanted to play. The boys had been in possession for some time and the girls had made up their minds to take over. Their technique was to have several girls torment the boys until they were chased; meanwhile, other girls moved into the coveted area.

Once the problem was out in the open the teacher asked, "What shall we do about it?" One child suggested that the teacher make a rule that nobody could play in this particular place at any time. "Would you like that?" the teacher questioned, and the children's answer was "no" because they did like to play there. A number of suggestions followed and were discussed pro and con. The final decision was that the children would take turns and that each group would play on some other part of the playground when the other occupied the priority spot.

At this point the teacher turned the discussion in another direction by saying, "This isn't our social studies period, but does this have anything to do with social studies or with some of the ideas we have talked about in social studies?" The subsequent discussion brought out these ideas: (1) We didn't exactly study anything for this, but we did learn something about some of the things we have talked about in social studies, like getting along with each other. (2) We think that sharing will give us more chance to play where we want than quarreling about it every day. (3) The playground belongs to everybody. (4) We have made a kind of rule to go by. (5) We have mostly figured this out for ourselves. (6) This is something like that word "cooperation" that was in the radio story the other day.

ANALYSIS OF THE EPISODE

What was the nature of the organizing center? In this situation it was a problem of real concern to the children. It had to be defined before it could be attacked. This step in itself is an important phase of problem solving often overlooked in practice.

There was opportunity for helping the group to move toward the achievement of the following social goals: (1) growth in self-control and self-direction, (2) respecting the rights of others, (3) discovering and meeting the group need of rules to live by, (4) working together co-operatively, and (5) solving problems through group interaction and the use of group ideas.[1] With guidance the children could see the relationship between solving their immediate problem and the goals previously discussed in connection with their social studies. It is perhaps at this point that teachers create for themselves a large measure of frustration. Because teachers fail to help them identify goals, children don't know where they are going, and teachers wonder why they aren't eager to get there.

It was important also to recognize that settlement of the problem was not final, that further problems and other facets of the same problem would arise, and that a way of solving group problems was being learned. The fact that the situation was not permanently taken care of does not mean that the process failed.

---

[1] Madison Public Schools, Curriculum Department, A Tentative Report of the Social Studies Committee of the Madison Public Schools (Madison, Wisconsin: Madison Public Schools, 1953).

Perhaps it is important for children to recognize and learn that final, satisfactory solutions to problems are not easily come by.

Where does this learning experience fit in the sequence definitions for the total social studies program and for this particular grade level?

Except in a program in which the immediate concerns of children determine the sequence of experiences, this episode has no particular place. However, it is typical of the sort of problem that arises every day. Since such problems are often of greater concern to children than many that teachers structure for them, they offer an excellent first-hand, ready-made medium for getting at important goals. Also—whether we desire it or not—when such problems arise, and they do arise, they are going to be solved somehow, and out of that solving children will acquire and practice some kind of group processes. What shall they be?

It is not argued that children be given full responsibility for solving problems nor that they be involved in the solutions of all problems. Some are beyond their understanding and pose too heavy a load. Even when they are solving those problems that are within their capabilities, they need to feel that the teacher is there to support and help them when needed.

In relating and analyzing this episode an attempt has been made to point out how everyday occurrences can become the centers for significant learning experiences and a help in achieving important social goals. It is more than "incidental learning." It doesn't just happen. It is the conscious use of the school-day events in directing learning toward defined goals.

PART THREE

A Method Of Curriculum Inquiry

As pointed out by Professor Herrick in Part I, content or subject matter can not be meaningfully separated from processes of inquiry. This is as true of curriculum theory as it is of any other areas of knowledge.

To develop and refine his ideas about curriculum design and instructional theory, Dr. Herrick frequently relied on actual classroom episodes as a source of raw data. These episodes were taped and transcribed in mimeograph form and were used by Dr. Herrick both as an instructional device and as material for his own inquiry into the nature of curriculum.

The purpose of the following selection is described by Dr. Herrick himself. Each of five graduate students developed a theoretical analysis of a classroom episode. These analyses are followed by a series of critiques written by Professor Herrick under the headings "The Results of Analysis for Episode A" and "Some Conclusions for Framework Building."

D. W. A.
J. B. M.
F. B. M.

11

Analysis Of Classroom Episodes

> *The intent in this chapter is to explore a number of ways to examine an episode, to discover what certain frameworks will show about this episode and, further, what this exercise will say about the nature and function of frameworks or structures in the whole process of curriculum thinking and theorizing.*
>
> *Virgil E. Herrick*

This working paper grows out of a series of exercises attempted by a graduate class in curriculum theory and design to try out different ways of looking at teaching-learning practices in the classroom. A number of assumptions undergirded these attempts:

1. Any instance of curriculum planning or teaching can be examined via a number of different bases which emphasize different aspects of the teaching act, different conclusions about the value of any particular phase, and, finally, different judgments as to what ought to be added or subtracted in order to form a coherent and comprehensive educational experience.

2. All frameworks for dealing with teaching episodes are not equally valuable, in that some consider particular aspects of the

teaching act and ignore others equally significant; some represent value orientations inconsistent with key concepts underlying the nature and essential function of American public education; some are more general or specific in general referent; some are frameworks which more clearly have to do with the essential tasks of all curricular planning and teaching than do others.

3. An adequate framework should have a number of particular characteristics:

    a. It should be sufficiently general to deal with episodes of different kinds, on different levels, and in different areas of the curriculum.

    b. It ought to serve more than a descriptive function. The framework should lead to some kind of positive valuing action in improving the teaching act represented in the episode.

    c. It should have the capacity to deal with both the planning and action phases of the teaching-learning act.

    d. It should enable the user to objectify for scrutiny, analysis, and possible revision the many internal and external dimensions of the teaching-learning act.

4. The task of building and using an adequate framework for examining, planning, and developing more adequate curriculum and teaching actions should at some point be the concern of every teacher and curriculum worker, and very likely, every learner, as this represents his metaknowledge about his developing education and life direction.

NATURE AND ROLE OF LEARNING EPISODES

It should be obvious to every worker in curriculum that it is very difficult to obtain both a source and a validating point for the development and testing of curriculum theory and design.

We have taken the position that records of actual teaching behavior form one important source for achieving this dual function. The assumptions underlying the use of a teaching episode are as follows:

1. Every episode is not an isolated bit of action: it exists in some educational and physical context; there is an antecedent and

a consequence but usually only the verbal portion of the action is recorded. (Some episodes are photographed and include the teaching plan of the teacher and some description of the previous experiences of the children in the area indicated.)

2. This incompleteness of an episode is not a disadvantage but actually a realistic condition in which the effective curriculum theorizing can take place. It permits consideration of all the possible alternatives and of what prior or subsequent knowledge is necessary to deal with choices in a certain way.

Actually, the above state of incompleteness represents accurately the realistic position of a teacher. He does not have access to all of the necessary data; he is constantly inferring from the behavior he observes the necessary data which he uses to change, modify, and redirect the action of the classroom; he is constantly applying some kind of perceptual, affective, and cognitive framework to his teaching acts.

3. The intent of this analysis is not to judge whether he is a good teacher or even whether the episode is a good educational experience. The intent here is to try to identify some of the common and necessary operations, patterns, and environments important in all teaching and curriculum planning, to try to understand more adequately what is happening, and to try to explore the different ways in which this episode could be modified to make it a more adequate educational experience. This last endeavor forces us to examine the bases upon which these value judgments are made.

4. Curriculum planning and the teaching act must be seen as clearly related aspects of the same essential task. Curriculum structures which do not lead directly to more effective educational action are as sterile as teaching actions which are not based on some kind of curricular theorizing.

5. The episode, in many cases, served as a springboard for as creative and open-minded an exploration as could be made by the individuals involved. Thus it is very likely that some professional liberties were taken with what might have been the "realities" of this recorded experience.

The specific episode was selected because it represented a limited, characteristically routine behavior found in every classroom. It lacks many of the resources found in other types of episodes recorded in the areas of social studies, science, mathematics, and the arts. It represents, therefore, an interesting test of the capabilities of these frameworks to deal with this limited kind of classroom experience. Another working paper will explore the usefulness of other kinds of frameworks for dealing with a lesson in one of the above subject areas.

Episode "A"

Teacher: "Now we will get ready for recess. People who are big enough to write their names are big enough to sit up. Girls, show the boys how still you can be while you get your coats. They're listening! Boys, now you show the girls."

 The children got their coats and other wraps, put them on, and sat down.

Teacher: "One." (The children turned to the side in their seats. Some children made the error of standing instead of merely turning. The teacher stopped counting and waited until those children reseated themselves.)

Teacher: "Two." (The children stood. One laggard was still putting on his coat. The teacher called the attention of the class to this child's slowness.)

Teacher: "Pass." (The children walked out of the room in single file.)

Presentation of Different Frameworks:
A Two-Level Structure
George O'Hearn

 The framework for this episode was derived from the simplicity and movement of the episode itself and was designed to fit the problem as it existed rather than make the problem conform to a foreign structure. Blooms *Taxonomy of Educational Objectives*[1] was useful for determining the levels of structure. Schwab's *Education and the Structure of*

---

[1] Benjamin S. Bloom, ed., *Taxonomy of Educational Objectives* (New York: David McKay, 1956) 207 pp.

a Discipline[2] and Bruner's *The Process of Education*[3] gave ideas and direction to the nature and purpose of any such structure, and the *Collected Papers* of V. Herrick[4] provided the needed background for thinking of the movement about the organizing centers.

The proposed structure (see Fig. 7) is dual in nature, with most of the activity and evaluation taking place on one level, whereas the other level, which is indeed important, is not well evaluated. The objectives or purposes of the actions produced by the teacher may be seen as twofold. The primary objective is the quiet and efficient exit of the pupils from the room to the play area. Secondary objectives are the training of students for obedience, respect of student group, spirit of competition, speed, and quietness, all of which are valued to some degree in our culture. The question of which of these objectives is to be called *primary* and which *secondary* depends on the person looking at the situation. I choose to look at it from the eyes of the teacher trying to empty the room for recess.

If we follow the indicated primary objectives, we find that the organizing center for the entire episode is the common act of getting ready for the passing to recess. All activity on both the primary and secondary level revolves about this goal. The process and content techniques include readying actions as well as the transitional actions. Class structure and management seem rigid and competitive. Boys are organized against girls for physical quietness and speed. Those individuals who do not conform are openly criticized. All of this is still revolving about the original organizing center—"to get ready for recess." On the secondary level the class structure and management influences many of the cognitive ideas formed.

The primary scope of the activity is limited and narrow, and it seems to be directed at the pupils' exit and nothing more. However, the secondary aspects of scope are broad and complex. Here we have children interacting with one another, being judged by a group of fellow students, and operating in a competitive atmosphere. There is much interaction between these primary and secondary objectives as move-

---

2 Joseph Schwab, "Education and the Structure of the Disciplines" *Educational Record*, July, 1962 (Washington, D. C.: The American Council of Education) pp. 197-205.

3 Jerome S. Bruner, *The Process of Education* (Cambridge, Massachusetts: Harvard University Press, 1960) 97 pp.

4 Virgil E. Herrick, *Collected Papers* (Madison, Wisconsin: College Printing Company, 1962) 220 pp.

ment takes place. The class movement is both physical—toward the
exiting objective—and intellectual (cognitive).

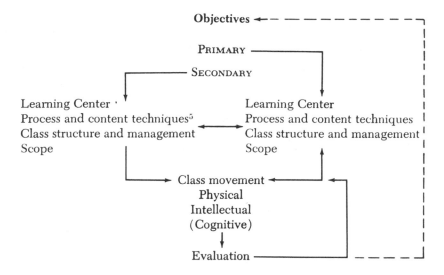

FIG. 7.   DIAGRAM OF A TWO-LEVEL STRUCTURE.

The students, because of their interaction with one another, the pressure
of their fellow students' judgment, and the keen spirit of competition,
develop an affective structure of needing to conform to group pressures.

This leads to an evaluation that is conducted mostly on the primary
level, since the activities on this level are easy to see, easy to judge, and,
in fact, lend themselves to immediate evaluation. If the group is orderly
and moves quietly and quickly, this will tend to reaffirm the mode of
movement shown by the solid line. A much less immediate evaluation
may lead back to the basic purpose, but this, I propose, will be an
indirect line of evaluation, as shown by the dotted line. Evaluation of
the secondary objectives and the attainment of these objectives in
general is not tested, but will manifest itself only in evaluation of the
physical movements.

---

[5] Members of the group have raised the question that this category includes values which, in effect, are a third category, or perhaps a third level of
consideration.

The proposed structure lends itself to an involved and yet logical analysis of the episode. Although the structure does not attempt to look in detail at all the aspects of the act, it does allow us to look at the relevant parts of the episode in as little or as much detail as we please and to separate the levels of activity. The sketch of this structure allows us at least to imply interactions and movements progressing throughout the episode.

This structure does not consider detailed psychological and social implications of the actions, although these could be added.

From this examinaton of the framework, it is possible to see both its adequacy and its inadequacy, but, even more importantly, one can see the utility and necessity for some such structure, a structure that not only gives direction to the act, but also isolates the important centers of activity and suggests their relevance to the objectives. With such a structure in mind, the evaluation of an episode takes on new meaning, since we now know what we are evaluating and how and where to apply these evaluative criteria to best elicit a change.

A Psychological Model
Sally True

The learning episode to be considered herein lends itself particularly well to a relationship to Kurt Lewin's field theory,[6] because this theory, that of hodological space or the science of paths, applies both literally and figuratively to the episode. One could say, that is, that the class is literally moving in space. Although it is the psychological meaning which Lewin intended, the circumstance of there being a congruence between physical and psychological movement seems to make the field theory apt for this analysis. In addition, the values operating within the episode do not appear to be democratic.

Model used for analysis

A brief description of Lewin's theory indicates that he conceived of the relating of topology, or the geometry of spatial relationships without regard to quantitative measurement, to the human psyche. Hodological space, as Lewin conceived it, was an extension of topology. It was

---

[6] Kurt Lewin, as described by Ernest R. Hilgard in *Theories of Learning* (New York: Appleton-Century-Crofts, 1956) pp. 258–89.

used to represent such dynamic concepts as direction, distance, force, and valence, applied to the human personality.

Lewin postulated the conception of the person moving and operating within life space. The person is organized into energy systems, with tensions and needs developing from internal conflicts and from frustrations in goal-seeking which act as motivating forces.

Other pertinent concepts are those of *valence* and *force*. *Valence* is the attraction or value which a particular region in life space holds for the individual. It is co-ordinated with a need. *Force* possesses the properties of direction, strength, and point of application, as Lewin conceived it. A force exists in the psychological environment. A tension exists in the inner-personal system of the individual. A *vector* is a representation of the length of the force and the strength and point of application of said force.

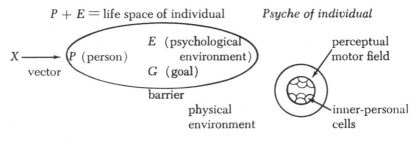

FIG. 8.   SUMMARY OF ELEMENTS IN LEWIN'S THEORY.

Application to episode

Each child will be considered a person-in-life-space (P). The teacher applies force in her first statement. The strength of the force shifts first to girls and then to boys. The point of application (i.e., the disposition of the psyche to which the teacher directs the force) is the child's desire for peer approval and approval from the authority figure.

Physical locomotion results as the children get their wraps. Psychological locomotion also results as tensions are developed in the inner systems because of the force which has been applied.

The teacher adds force when she begins counting. Her calling attention to the slow child adds strength to the force applied to this child. Again, both physical and psychological locomotion occur.

The valence in this episode is the desire of each child to please the teacher; that is, the valence is the approval given by the teacher. A barrier exists for the child who made the error of standing instead of merely turning. An even greater barrier exists for the slow child, because she is singled out for disapproval in front of the entire peer group. The inner tensions of this child will likely be severe. As an organism seeking to equalize tensions and to reach a homeostatic state, she may resort to overadaptive behavior on the playground (i.e., excessive hostility or withdrawal).

The basis of authority for the episode is force, given strength and direction by the teacher. The objective of the teacher is to get the class out to recess. The objective of the children is to escape reprimand.

The selection of what to do has been made entirely by the teacher's authority, with no regard for the inner-personal systems of the children. The organizing center is controlled throughout by the teacher.

Evaluation considered in terms of the objective (i.e., getting the children out to recess) would term the episode successful. In terms of what might be assumed to be the over-all objectives of the school, the episode is unsuccessful.

Lewin divides the psychological environment into regions in his theoretical model, stating that the number of regions is a function of the circumstances of life. A strong force can amalgamate all the regions into one. In this case, the force inspires fear which dominates the psychological environment of this classroom. All other considerations transformed from figure to ground as the dominant region of the life space of these children becomes that of fear and conformity.

By thus narrowing the field, this teacher has isolated this episode from the many complex and interrelated curriculum operations. In particular, she has neglected consideration of the needs of the learners and of democratic values.

Curricular considerations not covered

This framework does not take into consideration the content-process dimension of curriculum. The focus is upon the individual, his perceptions and his motivations. In addition, the focus is upon the group structure.

This theory appears to have no relation to the physical structures of the curriculum (e.g., instructional materials, resources, classrooms, school buildings, etc.).

A major criticism of field theory in general is that it is descriptive rather than predictive. This becomes a serious flaw in its use as a model for curriculum structure for the reason that a curricular model must give direction.

These considerations indicate that although Lewin's field theory is adequate to deal with some curricular operations, it is inadequate to deal with all of them. It is not sufficiently comprehensive to perform the necessary tasks required of curriculum structure.

An Analytical Model
John Maxwell

The framework was presented in Chapter 6 of *Language and Concepts in Education* by B. O. Smith and Robert H. Ennis.[7] The author of the chapter, Mr. Smith, borrowed the basic idea from E. C. Tolman's paradigm of learning:[8] *S-O-R*, itself a modification of the familiar *S-R* theory of learning. In Tolman's theory, and in Smith's framework, acts of a behavioral sort are triggered by a set of intervening variables which arise in the presence of certain stimuli. The intervening variables are *inferred* from observable actions; in a sense they are educated guesses about what occurs within the nervous system or mind of the subject. The basic form of the paradigm is as follows:

I	II	III
The independent variables (Teacher acts)	*Acting on the basis of inferred intervening variables*	*Move to produce certain dependent variables* (Pupil acts)
Linguistic behavior Performative behavior Expressive behavior	Pupil memories Beliefs Needs Inferences Associative mechanism	Linguistic behavior Performative behavior Expressive behavior

To illustrate, imagine that the teacher clears her throat in a warning way (I); various pupils stop wriggling or quickly check on their immediate behavior in some other way (II); we can infer that pupils, in the instant

---

[7] B. O. Smith and Robert H. Ennis, *Language and Concepts in Education* (Chicago: Rand McNally & Co., 1961).

[8] Edward C. Tolman, as described by Ernest R. Hilgard in *Theories of Learning* (New York: Appleton-Century-Crofts, 1956) pp. 185–221.

between the stimulus and their response (III), checked their memories for comparable situations and their need to avoid being "caught," and either inferred what their responding action ought to be or reacted automatically in an associative way.

The Smith article then states that the I, II order above can be instantly reversed at the completion of an overt action by the teacher. After a pupil action, the teacher then responds; but preceding the teacher action, a set of intervening variables occurs in the mind of the teacher. Thus, in horizonal form, a continuing classroom activity consists of a series of constantly reversing action patterns:

$$\ldots P_t\, D_t\, R_t \quad P_p\, D_p\, R_p \quad P_t\, D_t\, R_t \quad P_p\, D_p\, R_p \quad P_t \ldots \text{etc.}$$

where P_t = teacher perception of pupil behavior.
D_t = teacher diagnosis of pupil's state of interest.
R_t = teacher response, action based on diagnosis.

P_p = pupil perception of teacher behavior.
D_p = pupil diagnosis of teacher's state of interest.
R_p = pupil response, action on the basis of diagnosis of teacher behavior.

Double lines indicate the end of a teaching cycle; single lines separate the act of teaching from the act of taking instruction.

Application to episode

In the following application, the framework is presented in a descending vertical fashion, although it ought to be presented horizontally to symbolize the time-dimension continuum in which it occurs.

Phase	What is occurring
P_t	Teacher— perceives children watching clock, fidgeting, sitting up, folding hands.
D_t	Teacher— infers that pupils are remembering routine recess procedures as they anticipate recess.
R_t	Teacher— speaks: "Now we will get ready for recess;" stands, arms crossed on chest.

Phase		*What is occurring*
P_p	Pupils	— perceive waiting stature of teacher, as well as her words.
D_p	Pupils	— remember that teacher will wait for class to settle down and may use scorn or techniques of group pressure to enforce her request; will certainly delay departure until quieting comes.
R_p	Pupils	— respond by holding straight position in seats; some boys slow in responding.

P_t	Teacher—	sees class quieting, notes some boys not settling down.
D_t	Teacher—	infers that boys may not be completely willing to quiet down as the girls do.
R_t	Teacher—	(remembers previous success in improving responses from boys by placing them in competition with the girls) speaks: "Girls, show the boys how still you can be while you get your coats."

P_p	Pupils	— hear teacher's utterance; boys watch girls move to cloakroom; girls note resentment on boys' faces.
D_p	Pupils	— girls infer, "We are favored so long as we behave quietly;" boys, "This quietness business is important to teacher," or "Nuts to them. They aren't so smart. They are sissies."
R_p	Pupils	— girls continue their winning ways; boys force themselves into docility, but manage well-hidden sneers at returning girls.

P_t	Teacher—	perceives good behavior of girls; quieting effect on boys.
D_t	Teacher—	infers both groups have grasped her point; assumes both have remembered previous episodes of like form and have resolved in future to do better . . . .

And thus the ebb and flow of action and reaction continue throughout the passing incident. The paradigm is able to shed some light on the passing incident by focusing on the large part that inference and assumption play in the behavior of both teacher and pupils. Depending on the accuracy of the determination of what is going on in the mind of the other, each "side" can establish some basis for action. But the rigidity and one-sided nature of the "passing incident" presents an irony; the pupils actually seem to have a better set of inferences about the teacher than does the teacher about her pupils. Whether or not the pupils have learned from the situation depends on the relation between teacher diagnosis and *actual* intervening variables. A less rigid situation might give the teacher a better basis for inferring, but with children clamped so tightly under her thumb, her diagnosis is weakened for lack of meaningful data. Her procedures shut off sources and lines of data verification.

Generally, the usefulness of the analytical model for examining teacher and learning situations is marred by the excessively detailed kind of data which it produces. This particular application has examined a situation in a microscopic way, that is, almost at the level of high-speed, nearly instantaneous, reactions to stimuli. There is, within the framework as presented by Smith, little to prevent its being used in the microscopic way. Better use of the framework might employ a broader or macroscopic technique than I have used. For instance, the teacher act of giving an assignment would be perceived by the students as a whole act, stretching over several minutes' time. Then the pupil act of setting about the assignment could be viewed as a larger unit. Within both actions, perhaps, a vast number of small "ebbs-and-flows" units could be observed, but focus would be on the larger act.

The teacher might suggest, at this point, that this is a routine classroom action which should become habitual as soon as possible. Such routine procedures do not really involve diagnosis, only perception and response by the student.

In summary, if the Smith framework were used on complex teaching-learning situations, it is likely that the detailed analysis such as is presented on previous pages would not occur. This application treated a brief part of a short incident in which action was largely one-way. Unless a macrocosmic application were made, a complicated classroom situation would yield a mountain of data very difficult to handle.

An Operations-Communication Model
Tom Faix

I. BASIS OF THE MODEL USED

The purpose of the following was to hold up for inspection, analysis, and evaluation the key components of the teaching-learning act and at the same time develop an instrument with which to do it.

Too often in professional education we jump to value judgments based on our own particular, often inadequate, criteria, and our conclusions are often "fuzzy" and not explicit. To alleviate such approaches this framework necessitated looking "between the lines," or at the implicit assumptions of the episode.

II. PRESENTATION OF THE FRAMEWORK AND APPLICATION TO EPISODE "A"
The various dimensions are as follows:

A. *Objectives implicit for the teacher and pupils*
What were the teacher's *main* purposes?
1. To move the class physically to another activity.
2. To reinforce notions of obedience.
What were the teacher's *specific* purposes?
1. To develop notions of *quietness* as a positive behavior.
2. To develop notions of *listening* as a positive behavior.
3. To have children acquire and don wraps in preparation.
What were the pupil's *main* purposes?
1. To get out to recess as soon as possible.
What were the pupils' *specific* purposes?
1. To obey the teacher's directions.
2. To acquire and don wraps as directed.

B. *Organizing centers*
What were the main organizing centers used to achieve the objectives?

Cognitive (implicit)	*Process* (explicit)	*Attitude* (implicit)
1. Idea of recess.	1. Listening.	1. Recess is a privilege to be earned.
2. Idea of correct posture.	2. Self-correction.	2. Poor posture is childish behavior.
3. Idea of obedience.	3. Acting out directions given.	
4. Idea of competition.	4. Sex competition.	3. Not to obey holds everyone else up from recess.
5. Idea of orderly efficiency.	5. Acting out directions in given sequence.	4. Either boys *or* girls are naturally better.
		5. The best way to do things is for *everyone* to act at the same time.

C. *Communication interaction patterns*
What were the patterns of interaction or communication?

Ɔirect   Indirect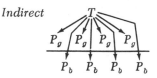

Combination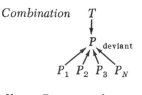

Key: P = pupil.
       g = girl.
       b = boy.
       T = teacher.

D. *Methods used and underlying learning theory assumptions*
What were the main methods and underlying assumptions of the teacher's behavior?

Method (explicit)	*Assumptions* (implicit)
1. Directive control.	1. Directive control.
a. Oral means to action.	a. The best way to expedite movement of pupils from room to recess is by a routine orderliness under teacher's oral direction.
b. Delaying the means to action.	b. All must conform; there is no room for deviation, or else all must suffer the wrong of a few.
c. Ridicule.	c. Children's behavior can be changed by pointing out their tendencies to regress toward childish behaviors.
d. Precise commands in sequence.	d. Children can be moved about from one place and function to another more quickly and more efficiently by using short direct clues.

2. Indirect control.   2. Indirect control.
   a. Sex competition.   a. Boys and girls are more
                                          likely to obey and improve
                                          their behavior if it can be
                                          proved that one sex is
                                          better than the other.
   b. Peer punishment.   b. Deviant children can be
                                          brought into line by
                                          having their behavior
                                          rejected by the peer group.

E. *Evaluation by teacher and pupils*
   What evaluation or reactions to the teaching-learning were in
   evidence?
   Teacher
   1. The teacher informed the class of her judgment of their
      actions.
   2. The teacher informed the class of the deviant action of some
      class members—an evaluation, by waiting for compliance.
   Pupils
   1. The pupils had learned what these judgments would be
      from previous experience with this teacher.
   2. The pupils were to evaluate their own behavior by the
      standard of being "childish" or being "grown-up."
   3. The pupils were to evaluate their own behavior and that of
      their peer group by the standard of whether or not they
      held up the action of the group.
   4. The entire class behavior was evaluated by how soon they
      were allowed to go out to recess.
   5. The one deviant was to evaluate his action by the standard
      of how well and how promptly he conformed to the peer
      group and to teacher expectations.

F. *Philosophies of teaching implicit*
   These teacher behaviors are characteristic of an authoritarian
   personality, given to highly directive methods, with a corresponding rigid notion of child development and behavior. There
   seems also a rather narrow dated conception of how learning
   takes place.

G. *Summary statement drawing value judgments*
   In context *1* above, this classroom could be seen as highly
   repressed and not conductive to wholesome learning experience.

III. ADEQUACY OF THE STRUCTURE USED
This framework seemed adequate to get down to the bedrock of the underlying nature of this episode. There is, however, a main dimension or component that was neglected.

Possible affective environments and implications of each

In other words, a vital dimension, the emotional climate of this particular classroom, was missing. Therefore, we should have first examined it with an assumption that the climate was "cold, unsupportive, repressed." This was done here, but what also should have been done was to analyze the episode from the viewpoint of a climate of "repressed joy, eagerness, excitement" of pupils who were close to their teacher. It can be seen that the value judgment placed on the episode in the latter case would have been quite different.

This affective (emotional) environment may also have been influenced by the time of day, the weather, the physical arrangement of the desks, the socio-economic neighborhood, the particular mood of the teacher or class that day, or one of many possible personality patterns teachers may reflect. It can be seen that this additional vital component would add considerable more work to such analysis but get at much more realism.

It would also seem, since we can only infer possible affective environments, that it is really impossible to draw any meaningful value judgments on the episode by way of summary statements.

A Curriculum Model
Evelyn Weber

I. *Basis for the Selection of the Framework*
The rationale for the development of this model for the analysis of routine procedures in the classroom is simplicity itself. The episode being used and the various components were singled out and put into a meaningful relationship. Hopefully, this placing of elements into a pattern of relationship was expected to highlight the import of the learnings inherent in the situation.

The components seemed to fall under four major headings: objectives, group interaction, process, and learning outcomes. To complete the picture and to test the consequences of the learnings for pupils, the aspect of evaluation involving the total episode was added.

Objectives. The teacher obviously had a direct purpose, to get children out of the classroom and onto the playground; but, even more significantly, the implicit, long-term purposes of the teacher may be deduced from the episode.

Group interaction. A large component of every classroom situation is the interaction of group members, which includes some kind of leadership, organization, and a rate of procedure with a resultant classroom atmosphere.

Process. Process is a necessary element, providing for motivation and accounting for either an easy flow of activity from one step to another, or for intermittent, sporadic activity, dependent upon continual direction.

Learning outcomes. As the analysis later shows, the learning outcomes are a result of the other three elements: objectives, interaction, and process.

One notion was very consciously built into this model. This was the wish of the writer to look at all elements of the learning episode quite objectively, before any judgmental aspects entered into the framework. Thus, evaluation was quite logically made the final step. (It is clear, however, that we begin making certain tentative judgments the moment we start using a framework.)

II. *The Model and Its Application to the Episode*
    The model and its use in the analysis of the episode follows.

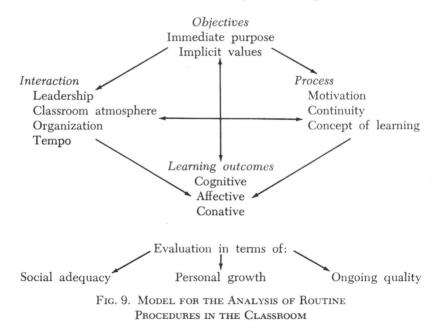

FIG. 9. MODEL FOR THE ANALYSIS OF ROUTINE
PROCEDURES IN THE CLASSROOM

Using the Model to Analyze the Episode

Objectives

Immediate purpose
To get group of children
out to recess.
Implicit Values
Quiet and order.
Following of directions.
Immediate obedience.
Conformity.

Interaction

Leadership
All invested in the teacher.
Teacher does all communicating,
purposing, evaluating.
No room for child initiative
or response.
Classroom Atmosphere
Teacher's purpose for group
dominates.
Little respect for individual
children's needs, purposes,
or natural tempo.
Organization
All children doing same
thing—rigidly.
No room for deviation.
Tempo
All proceed at same speed.
Hurried.
Forced action.

Process

Direction
Imitation
Lock-step Procedure
Motivation
Normative action on part of
teacher.
Appeal to maturity.
Peer group standards.
Competition between sexes.
Disapproval clues given by
teacher.
Continuity
Each step discrete.
Next step can't be carried
out without further
command.
Concept of Learning
Children learn social behavior
by being told what to do.

Possible Learning Outcomes

Cognitive
Must follow teacher's directions.
Lack of response brings disapproval,
sarcasm, being held up to class
ridicule.

Conformity is more feasible than individual
reactions.
Competition of the sexes is more important
than co-operation.
Slowpokes and nonconformists delay us in
getting out to recess.
Affective
Dislike of teacher or the school.
Lack of respect for opposite sex.
Dislike of slow pokes and nonconformers.
Conative
Just wait—teacher will tell you what to do.
No need to make own decisions.

Evaluation

Social Adequacy

Promotes dependence on
direction rather than
independence and responsibility
necessary in a democratic
society.
Develops competitive, rather
than co-operative, spirit.
Children grow in democratic
process of purposing, planning,
evaluating.

Personal Growth

No provision for children to
develop more adequate self
concepts.
No provision for children to
see their sex role more
clearly.
No provision for individual
differences in performance.

Continuity
No relationship to a group of
people in a natural situation.
No possible transfer to life
situation.

The application of the model to the episode reveals that it rather
successfully allows the reader to view the situation in each of its component parts and as a totality. However, since the framework was built
around a particular episode, the writer was interested in its effectiveness
in the analysis of other episodes. The usefulness was tested by applying
it to an episode with quite a different set of values, concept of learning,
and interaction pattern.

The second episode and the application of the model to it follow. This test demonstrated the worth of the model more clearly.

A New Episode
Another Way to deal with Routine Procedures in School

Jim: "It's 10:15. That's the time we planned to go out to recess."

Mary: "I would like to finish my part of the mural before I go."

Jim: "So would I."

Mary: "Miss Williams, may Jim and I stay in until we finish this part?"

Miss Williams: "How much more do you have to do?"

Mary: "Just this small bit."

Miss Williams: "All right. That's fine." (To entire group) "Jim reminds us that it is recess time. Why don't the children working on individual projects finish their immediate task, put things away, and then get ready and go outside? How far along is the group working on planning the costumes for our play?"

Paul: "Not very far. We'll have to work on them again tomorrow."

Miss Williams: "Then it sounds as if you are ready to go out to recess. Remember, boys and girls, that the first grade class has visitors today, so there is a special need for quiet in the halls."

Children finish tasks, put things away, consult the teacher about some things, and then leave the room individually or in small groups. Some remain for some time until task is completed.

USING MODEL TO ANALYZE SECOND EPISODE

Objectives
Immediate purpose
To move from individual and small group
activities to outdoor recess.
Implicit Values
Quiet and order.
Building individual responsibility.
Building children's judgment.
Respect for individual interests and needs.

Interaction	*Process*
Leadership	Teacher-pupil Planning
Shared by teacher and pupils.	Motivation
Both involved in communicat-	Consideration for others.
ing, purposing.	Interest in ongoing activities.
Teacher facilitating action.	Ongoing Quality
Classroom Atmosphere	Continuous.
Individual and group purposes	Children can move from one
involved.	activity to another without
Relaxed, accepting.	new direction.
Respect for individual children.	Concept of Learning
Organization	Children learn best by practice
Children working on individual	rather than precept.
or on small group projects.	
Opportunity for individual	
interests and skills.	
Tempo	
Children have opportunity to	
proceed at own pace.	
Natural.	
In control.	

Possible Learning Outcomes

Cognitive
  Children and adults can plan together.
  We don't all have to work at the same speed.
  It is good to respect and consider others.

Affective
  Satisfaction in completing a task before beginning a new
    activity.
  School is a comfortable place for all to work.

Conative
  It is important to have your own ideas and make your own
    decisions.

Evaluation

Social Adequacy	*Personal Growth*
Develops sense of personal ade-	Individual differences developed.
quacy and responsibility nec-	Opportunity for children to develop
essary in a democracy.	many skills.
Children have opportunity to de-	
velop skills of group action.	

Ongoing Quality
Very similar to normal group life situation

III. *Strengths and Weaknesses of the Framework*

The model appears to be useful in the analysis of these classroom episodes; first, in promoting the objective viewing of what went on, and second, in providing a means for evaluating them in their entirety. The writer then turned to the worth of the model for a classroom teacher in planning a learning situation. The question arose, "Should there be two models, one for analysis and one for planning?" Parsimony would suggest a single model. Further, one model would promote communication between teachers and those interested in analysis.

From the point of view of the teacher's planning, one omission in the model is the identification of the source of objectives. The framework also has no place for designating the organizing centers of the episode. The decisions related to the vehicles used to organize learning experiences with a group of children have great practical significance. The addition of this aspect would enhance its usefulness to the teacher, since these centers carry the classroom action.

The model was built around a routine situation involving no subject-matter content. This is an element that needs consideration in the expansion of its utility to other kinds of episodes. Later work with the model revealed that it could rather easily be adjusted to include these missing elements in its structure.

THE RESULTS OF
ANALYSIS FOR EPISODE "A"

As one reads the attempts to apply various models to the analysis, he is impressed with the amount that could be said about this brief routine episodic moment in the life of a teacher and a group of children. Since many of these comments are based on inferences drawn from limited data, this summary will be organized around major headings which represent those aspects which are highlighted by the five analyses contained in this working paper. The reader should, therefore, test these categorical headings in his own thinking to see if they are, in fact, the important aspects to be considered in any act of curriculum planning and teaching. He also should consider critically what is said in order to see if it represents sound applications of recognized educational values that are consistent with the emergent well-documented knowledge of the related supporting fields.

It is the thesis of this working paper that these admittedly incomplete and imperfect models have led to a consideration of this limited teaching act on a basis more adequate than most of those commonly found in the professional literature and practice.

I. *Relation of the limited purpose of physical movement to personal and social values and processes*

O'Hearn, Weber, and Faix point out the relationship of a more limited purpose "to get the children out to recess quickly and quietly" to longer-time purposes and considerations which have to do with developing independence, co-operative social action, concern for self-respect, and increased ability to deal with such developmental tasks as gaining one's own self concept and sex role, living with one's own peers, and winning some independence from the adults with whom he lives.

The major curricular points made were that every episodic situation in a classroom has to concern itself with multiple kinds of objectives, and that sometimes the way in which the immediate and short-range objective is achieved has a great deal to do with how the long-range objectives are obstructed or realized. Too great efficiency in achieving a specific and limited purpose may lead to inefficiency and obstacles to achieving the broader outcomes of the quality of responsibleness and self-direction desired. The ideal is to move routine matters as rapidly as possible into the sphere of control of children.

The use of such models revealed clearly, as the above comments indicate, that the routine procedures of a classroom and school cannot be considered in isolation from the total program of a school. Certain values and respect patterns should not be promoted in the social studies class and yet neglected in the routines for passing to recess.

II. *Nature of the forces and signs which are used to generate and direct behavior*

Maxwell's and True's analyses, as do most of the others, point out well that this teacher is introducing clues for behaving one at a time and as she sees the need for moving the action along. She reinforces and pushes this action with such forces as shaming the slow child and the child who moves too soon, with competition between boys and girls, with identifying correct actions with the concept of "big" boys and girls, and with the desire of all the children to please the teacher. Weber's reconstruction of the episode shows how other kinds of incentives might be used.

III. *The nature of the organizing centers and the temporal sequences introduced and controlled by the teacher*

All discussants concerned themselves with the nature of the bases the children had for organizing and directing their own behavior. It was pointed out that such words as "ready for recess," "one," "two," "pass" were used by the teacher to initiate and focus various phases of the action. Between these centers, the teacher asked the children to look at slow and out-of-phase children for the purpose of applying certain forces which would redirect their behavior.

These centers, with the exception of the slow children, were signs which had little meaning of their own (other than sequential) and to which all different kinds of behavior could be attached at the pleasure of the teacher. This forced the action to be of the conditioning nature that it was. Until the teacher revealed what behavior she wanted attached to these organizing centers, even the most able child would not know what it was.

A second point made by the analyses had to do with the temporal sequence of such centers. This sequence was controlled by the teacher, and each phase was introduced on the basis of the feedbacks she obtained from her observation of the children's behavior.

IV. *The nature of the communication system used*

Faix centered his examination of the episode in the communication system used. His discussion extends and reinforces the points previously made: it is one-sided—controlled exclusively by the teacher; the feedbacks were available to her but not to the children; little meaningful data was available to the learner in order to make his participation in the communication model a more meaningful one.

Maxwell, on the other hand, holds that the pupil being "more lost" had to work harder to infer meaning of the stimuli presented one at a time by the teacher.

Faix also goes on and examines the inferences and assumptions underlying the communication procedures used.

V. *The cognitive meanings of this experience*

O'Hearn, Maxwell, and Weber make the point, which supports Faix's analysis, that, besides getting physical bodies out to recess, many ideas not perceived by the teacher are being gained by these children about many important things. These ideas have to do with their self concept, how things are handled by adults in their world, what they need to learn in order to get along; maturity is associated with certain kinds of behavior and not with others, and the like.

Until this is examined, few teachers are aware of the concepts implicit in many of their routine procedures which seem to be easy ways to achieve limited purposes.

VI. *Teacher's and children's roles*

True, Maxwell, and Weber elaborated on the roles of the teacher and children. True focused on the life space of the individual and his goal-seeking behaviors, the valences inherent in what he does as a learner or as a teacher and what this implies. The role of the teacher is seen as authoritarian and the children's role as one of conforming. Maxwell examines the perceiving and inferring actions of teachers and pupils, using these as a basis for defining their role perceptions. Weber examines these roles in relation to what the teacher sees herself doing.

The major point made is that the conception the teacher has of her role sets the way in which she will tend to handle many kinds of routine situations in her teaching. Perhaps role conception is the basis of teacher style.

VII. *The explicit and implicit value positions assumed by the teacher*

One of the significant outcomes of this exercise in model application is the extent to which the five participants all used their models, which were relatively "value-free," to examine the value frames which supported the teacher's action and then to examine other alternative value frames which would direct the development of similar episodes in different directions. Weber went so far as to reconstruct the episode in a different way and then to see if her model would pick up these differences in value position.

SOME CONCLUSIONS
FOR FRAMEWORK BUILDING

The purpose of this working paper was to see if we could understand more adequately the nature and function of frameworks or structures in dealing with problems of curriculum development. Our experience seemed to indicate the following generalizations as being important:

1. All of the present structures were incomplete at some point.

Each model had value at the point where it made its major contribution. O'Hearn's contribution—two-level; True's—the individual and his topological space; Maxwell's—assumptions and inferences; Faix's—communication pattern; and Weber's—curricular decisions were on different levels of specificity and conclusiveness. True's was the most focused; Weber's was the most inclusive.

Each model had its lacks. In some, consideration of the social-emotional climate was missing; in others, educational objectives; and in others, the organizing centers which provided the vehicles for the educational movement.

The positive direction which seemed to emerge is that the personality, learning, and communication models need to be placed in some educational situation, rather than vice-versa.

2. The importance of the concept of transaction.

The examination of each model and its application to episode "A" showed that as the person using the model could find useful dimensions which were common to both the model and episode "A," then the analysis and interpretation of the episode took on greater power as the directives of the model could be *transacted* to the episode and vice-versa. Inferences and generalizations were drawn with greater clarity and specificity of reference.

The second aspect of this idea of transaction as an essential attribute of a good design is the importance of any analysis' going beyond the specific episode to the ways in which it should be changed in order that greater educational value could be obtained.

The third idea of transaction important in a model is the capacity of the model to transact the relationships which ought to result when one moves from consideration of one phase of a model to another. It was abundantly clear in the analysis of episode "A" that consideration of value frames had a great deal to say about teacher-pupil roles, communication patterns, organizing centers, and the like. Similarly, a consideration of the forces and life-space phenomena had something to say about teacher roles, objectives, and communication patterns.

A fourth idea of transaction is the importance of movement from a specific act or episode to the larger context of acts or episodes within which the specific becomes understandable.

These four ideas of the capacity of a model for movement in a number of important directions seem to lie at the heart of the usefulness of any framework for dealing with problems of curriculum planning and development.

3. The need for value referents.

The action and usefulness of each model grew as it used one or a number of different value referents for considering the action of the episode. Each person, in using his model, intended more than merely describing what happened. Some did little more than to pull out what they considered to be critical areas of behavior; others started to introduce such objectives as value directions, co-operative rather than competitive social processes, maximizing learner role rather than teacher role, flexible and permissive exploration of procedures rather than restrictive and limited proscription.

There seemed to be some evidence to show that a curriculum model based on common teaching operations which permitted the exploration of the consequences of a number of different value frames seemed to have greater long-time value than a more restrictive model with its own built-in value referents (not a conclusion—a proposition to be verified by more study).

4. The utility of some kind of structure.

The experience of this group exploring the values of models in dealing with curriculum planning and teaching practice shows the real value of some framework for exploring the complicated and extensive domain of curriculum and teaching.

Each model, no matter how limited and incomplete, permitted its user to say something important about the episode and to suggest ways to improve it. Such frameworks suggest important areas to consider, point up necessary relationships between parts, and provide the dimensions and value-referent considerations for acting directly upon the task at hand—understanding and improving our curriculum planning and resulting teaching action.

In closing, Maxwell's caution is well taken. "[In the episode] . . . high-speed, nearly instantaneous reactions were made to stimuli—yet we analyzed it in microscopic ways. There is need for macroscopic applications to be made . . . in order to see how the vast number of ebbs and flows could be observed in the context of fewer, more significant, larger acts . . . [otherwise,] a complicated classroom situation will yield impossible mountains of data."

Credits

Chapter 1   *Collected Papers.* Madison, Wisconsin: College Printing Company, 1962, 220 pp.

Chapter 2   The first four paragraphs of this selection are from an unpublished paper. The remaining part of the selection is from a chapter by the same title in the monograph: Herrick, Virgil and Tyler, Ralph, *Toward Curriculum Theory.* Chicago: University of Chicago Press, 1950.

Chapter 3   From "Planned and Unplanned Curriculum," *Elementary School Journal,* 47 (June, 1947), pp. 565–70.

Chapter 4   From *Collected Papers.*

Chapter 5   An original paper, later published in *Proceedings of Nature of Teaching Conference.* Milwaukee, Wisconsin: University of Wisconsin, October, 1962.

Chapter 6   From *Collected Papers.*

Chapter 7   Herrick et al., *The Elementary School.* Englewood Cliffs, New Jersey: Prentice-Hall, Inc., 1956, pp. 107–12.

Chapter 8   Pages 114–21 are from *Collected Papers.* Pages 121–24 are from *N.S.S.E. Yearbook.* The remainder of the chapter is from *Collected Papers.*

Chapter 9   From *Collected Papers.*

Chapter 10   Estvan, F.J., Herrick, Virgil, and Steele, Jessie Knapps, "Experiences for Achieving Social Goals," *Social Education of Young Children,* Mary Willcockson, ed. National Council for the Social Studies, Curriculum Series No. 4, 1956, pp. 29–33.

Chapter 11   Unpublished paper, University of Wisconsin, 1962.

Biography

Virgil E. Herrick

Degrees

University of Wisconsin
B.A. 1929 with honors
M.A. 1930 Education
Ph.D. 1936; awarded Sterling Fellowship for graduate study.

Professional Positions

Principal and teacher, Washington Junior High School, Berlin, Wisconsin	1925–27
Director of Guidance and Curriculum, and teacher, Milwaukee Country Day School, Milwaukee, Wisconsin	1930-38
Director, University of Wisconsin Laboratory School	Summer, 1938
Instructor, University of Wisconsin	Summer, 1936
Assistant Professor and Director of Reading Clinic, Syracuse University	1938–40
Assistant and Associate Professor, University of Chicago	1940–48
Professor of Education, University of Wisconsin	1948–63

Professional Recognitions

Vilas Professorship	1962
Chairman, School of Education Committee on Development of Program for Preparation of Elementary School Teachers	1949–51
Program accepted by University Faculty and Board of Regents	1951
Member, Graduate School Research Committee	1950–60
Chairman, Committee on Research in Basic Skills	1952–63
Co-chairman, Committee on Curriculum, American Association of College Teachers of Education	1946–48
Educator in Residence, University of Texas	Summer, 1956
President of American Educational Research Association	1957–58

Editorial board, *Journal of Teacher Education*	1958–61
Editorial board, *Elementary School Journal*	1942–49
National Award, Outstanding Research in Hand- writing, Handwriting Foundation	1959
Carnegie Lecturer, Behavorial Sciences and Curriculum Theory, Northwestern University Symposium on Psychology and Education	1959
Chairman, Educational Committee Handwriting Foundation	1961

Consultant Service

Directed survey of programs in elementary education, Chicago Public Schools	1958–59
Directed surveys of Oak Park, Barrington, Highland Park, Grand Rapids, Battle Creek, University of Chicago	1945–48
Consultant, Milwaukee Public Schools	1955–63
Consultant, Kellogg Foundation	1940–42
Consultant, The La Grange Study of In–Service Education	1945–48

Research Grants

University of Chicago, Graduate School
University of Wisconsin, Graduate School
Rockefeller Foundation
Parker Pen Company
U. S. Office of Education
National Institute of Mental Health
Handwriting Foundation

Bibliography

(This bibliography does not include published notes or book reviews.)

Research and Professional Books

Eells, Davis, Havighurst, Herrick, and Tyler, *Intelligence and Cultural Differences: A Study of Cultural Learning and Problem Solving.* Chicago: University of Chicago Press, 1951, 388 pp.
Chosen one of the fifty most significant books on Education in 1952.

Herrick, Virgil E., *Issues in Elementary Education.* Burgess Publishing Co., June 1952, 225 pp.

_____ and Jacobs, Leland, *Children and the Language Arts.* Englewood Cliffs, N.J.: Prentice-Hall, Inc., 1955, 524 pp.
Selected as one of the fifty best educational books in 1955.

_____, et al., *The Elementary School.* Englewood Cliffs, N.J.: Prentice-Hall, Inc., 1956, 635 pp.
Selected as one of the fifty best educational books in 1957.

_____, and Tyler, Ralph, *Toward Improved Curriculum Theory.* Chicago: University of Chicago Press, March, 1950, 124 pp.
Regarded as a basic reference in the field of curriculum theory.

_____, et al., *Providing for Individual Differences in the Elementary School.* Englewood Cliffs, N.J.: Prentice-Hall, Inc., 1960, 278 pp.

_____ ed., *New Horizons for Research in Handwriting.* Madison, Wisconsin: University of Wisconsin Press, June, 1962, 400+ pp.

Research and Professional Monographs

Herrick, Virgil E. and Fowlkes, John Guy, *Character Education.* Madison, Wisconsin: Department of Education, University of Wisconsin, 1930.

_____, *Handbook for Studying an Elementary School Program.* Chicago: Department of Education, University of Chicago Press, 1943.

_____, *Manual for Case Studies in Remedial Reading.* Syracuse, N.Y.: Department of Education, Syracuse University Bookstore, 1939.

_____, ed. and chapter contributor, *The Educational Program: Early and Middle Childhood.* Review of Educational Research, April, 1953.

_____, *The Design of a Writing Instrument.* Madison, Wisconsin: Department of Education, University of Wisconsin, October, 1953, 203 pp.

_____ and Macdonald, James, *The Preferences of Children and Adults for Common Writing Instruments.* Madison, Wisconsin: Department of Education, University of Wisconsin, October, 1953, 67 pp.

_____, ed. *Pressure Patterns in Handwriting*. Madison, Wisconsin: School of Education Bulletin, University of Wisconsin, March, 1955, 70 pp.

_____, et al., *Handwriting in Wisconsin: A Survey of Elementary School Practice*. Madison, Wisconsin: Bulletin of School of Education, University of Wisconsin, October, 1951, 77 pp.

_____, *Comparison of Practices in Handwriting Advocated by Nineteen Commercial Systems of Handwriting Instruction*. Madison, Wisconsin: Department of Education, University of Wisconsin, July, 1960, 111 pp.

_____, et al., *Children's Writing: Research in Composition and Related Skills*. Monograph, National Council of Teachers of English, 1960, 73 pp.

_____, et al., *Parent-Teacher Conference*. Fond du Lac Press, 1956, 65 pp.

_____, *Comprehensive Bibliography of Handwriting and Related Factors, 1890–1960*. Washington, D.C.: Handwriting Foundation, 1961, 108 pp.

_____ and Okada, Nora, *National Survey of Handwriting Practices*. Madison, Wisconsin: Department of Education, University of Wisconsin, 1962, 125 pp.

_____ and Nerbovig, Marcella, *The Improvement of Experience Chart Writing*. San Francisco, California: Howard Chandler, 1962, 95 pp.

_____, Harris, Theodore L., and Rarick, G. Lawrence, *The Perception of Skill Behavior: Handwriting*. Washington, D.C.: U. S. Office of Education, July, 1961, 225 pp.

_____ and Paukner, Lillian, *Milwaukee's Children Learn to Write*. Milwaukee, Wisconsin: Board of Education, Milwaukee Public Schools, 1960, 81 pp.

_____ and Otto, Wayne, *Letter Form Models Advocated by Commercial Handwriting Systems*. Madison, Wisconsin: School of Education, University of Wisconsin, August, 1960, 40 pp.

Chapters in Research and Professional Books and in Yearbooks of Professional Societies

Herrick, Virgil E., "Program of Inservice Education," 14th Annual Conference Proceedings, *Forthcoming Developments in American Education*. Chicago: Department of Education, University of Chicago Press, 1945.

_____, "Nature of Basic Techniques of Adjustment in Providing for Individual Differences and Needs." Proceedings of Conference on Reading, *Adjusting Reading Programs to Individuals*. Chicago: Department of Education, University of Chicago Press, 1941.

_____, "Nature of and Techniques Involved in Cooperative Effort in Schools to Improve Reading." Proceedings of Conference on Reading, *Comparative Effort in Schools to Improve Reading*. Chicago: Department of Education, University of Chicago Press, 1942.

_____, "Challenge of Poor Readers and Basic Principles Underlying Their Identification." Proceedings of Conference on Reading, *Adjusting Reading Program to Wartime Needs*. Chicago: Department of Education, University of Chicago Press, 1942.

_____, "Developing a Curriculum for a Democratic Social Order." 13th Annual Conference for Administrative Officers of Public and Private Schools, *Significant Aspects of American Life and Postwar Education*. Chicago: Department of Education, University of Chicago Press, 1944.

_____, "School and the Improvement of Education in Rural Communities." *Education in Rural America*, F. W. Reeves, ed. Chicago: University of Chicago Press, 1946.

_____ and Estvan, Frank J., "Evaluation of Skills in Social Studies." 1953 Yearbook of National Council of Social Studies Teachers, *The Development of the Social Studies Skills* (November, 1953).

_____, "The Selection of Learning Experiences with Young Children." National Council of Social Studies Monograph on *Social Studies Program for Young Children*, June, 1947.

_____ and Steele, Jessie, "The Selection of Experiences to Achieve Social Goals." Chap. III, National Council of Social Studies Monograph on *Social Studies Program for Young Children*. Revised edition, June, 1954.

_____, "Evaluation of Change in Programs of Inservice Education." Chapter in NSSE Yearbook, *Inservice Education*, 1957.

_____ and Harris, Chester, "Handling Data in Curriculum Research." Chapter in ASCD Yearbook, *Research for Curriculum Development*, 1957.

_____, "Review of *Iowa Every Pupil Basic Skills Test and Standard Achievement Test Battery*," Oscar Burros, *Mental Measurement Yearbook*, 1959, pp. 8–15.

_____, *The Evaluation of Reading*, University of Chicago Educational Monographs, *The Evaluation of Reading Instruction*, December, 1958.

_____, Chap. 3 in *Curriculum Design*. Review of Educational Research (Curriculum and Instruction), June, 1957.

_____, "Elementary Education: The Program," 3rd edition, *Encyclopedia of Educational Research*. New York: The Macmillan Company, 1960, pp. 430–442.

_____, "Curriculum Design." *Review of Educational Research*, XXX, No. 3 (June, 1960).

_____, "Basal Instructional Materials in Reading," *NSSE Yearbook on Reading*, Chap. X, November, 1960.

_____ et al. Chapter in *Contribution of Behavioral Science to Curriculum Theory*, James Macdonald, ed. School of Education, University of Wisconsin-Milwaukee, 1961, 96 pp.

_____ et al., "Administrative Structures and Processes in Curriculum Development." *Curriculum Planning and Development*, Review of Educational Research, June, 1960.

_____, "University Responsibility for Education of Staff in Educational Research" (Paper used in three five-day seminars on educational research, University of North Carolina, University of Chicago, University of California-Berkeley). Published in *Proceedings NASA*, 1961.

_____, "Practices in Teaching of Handwriting in U.S.: 1960," Chapter in *New Horizons in Research in Handwriting*, Madison, Wisconsin: University of Wisconsin Press, June, 1962.

_____, "The Evaluation of Quality in Handwriting," Chapter in *New Horizons in Research in Handwriting*. Madison, Wisconsin: University of Wisconsin Press, June, 1962.

_____ and Harris, Theodore, "The Perception of Handwriting Symbols," Chapter in *New Horizons in Research in Handwriting*. Madison, Wisconsin: University of Wisconsin Press, June, 1962.

_____, "The Future of Off Campus Programs," Chap. VII *Off Campus Student Teaching*, 1951.

Published and Mimeographed Research and Theoretical Papers

Herrick, Virgil E., *Bases for Planning Programs of Elementary Education* (mimeographed). University of the State of New York, Department of Public Instruction, Albany, New York, January, 1939.

_____, *The Work of the Consultant* (mimeographed). W. V. Kellogg Foundation, Battle Creek, Michigan, September, 1942.

_____ and Sewell, William, *A Proposed Program of Research Training in Social Behavior* (typewritten), for Faculty Seminar on Research Training (supported by SSRC), February, 1953.

_____, *The Role of a University in Programs of Field Study* (mimeographed), Committee on Field Studies, Department of Education, University of Chicago, August, 1944.

_____ et al., *The Development of a Workshop Program* (mimeographed), Department of Education, University of Chicago, July, 1945.

_____, *Introduction to Elementary Education*. Madison, Wisconsin: Department of Education, University of Wisconsin, September, 1955, 185 pp.

_____, *Problems of Research in Curriculum Design* (mimeographed), Panel on Curriculum Research, AERA, Atlantic City, February, 1957, 28 pp.

_____, *Educational Objectives and Evaluation*, Commission on Instruction, N.E.A. May, 1959.

_____, *Ten Years of Research in Handwriting* (mimeographed), Department of Education, University of Wisconsin, August, 1959.

————, *Needed Curriculum Theory in Teacher Education.* Paper presented to Conference on Needed Publications in Teacher Education, New York City, November, 1960.

————, *Cooperative Research.* Paper presented to Big Ten Research Coordinators, University of Chicago, November, 1960. Published in *Proceedings,* Egon Guba, editor.

————, *Leadership Responsibilities of Principals for Instruction* (mimeographed), Administrative Personnel and Superintendents, Chicago Public Schools, December, 1961.

————, *The Development of Leadership in Programs of Curriculum Development* (mimeographed), Starved Rock Conference, State of Illinois Department of Public Instruction, October, 1961.

————, *Principles Underlying Cooperative Research,* Committee on Inter-institutional Research, Big Ten and University of Chicago, Northwestern University, June, 1961. Printed in *Proceedings.*

————, *Collected Papers.* Madison, Wisconsin: College Printing Co., 1962, 220 pp.

Research and Professional Articles

Herrick, Virgil E., and Luberg, Leroy, "University Laboratory School," *Wisconsin Journal of Education,* September, 1938.

————, "Selecting the Child in Need of Special Reading Instruction," *The Elementary School Journal,* February, 1940.

————, "Present Problems Facing the Elementary School: First Report," *The Elementary School Journal,* May, 1942.

————, "Knowing our Neighbors," *The Elementary School Journal,* November, 1941.

————, "Research in Vocabulary Development," *The Elementary School Journal,* December, 1957.

————, "Present Pressures on the Elementary School," *The Elementary School Journal,* November, 1942.

————, "Values in Elementary School Teaching," *The Elementary School Journal,* November, 1943.

————, "Obstacles to Teacher-Pupil Planning in the Elementary School," *The Elementary School Journal,* September, 1942.

————, "Adjustment Counseling with Teachers," *Educational Administration and Supervision,* March, 1944.

————, "Present Problems Facing the Elementary School," *The Elementary School Journal,* May, 1943; "A Second Report," June, 1944.

_____, "Development of Understanding Among Men," *The Elementary School Journal,* November, 1944.

_____, "Religion in the Public Schools of America," *The Elementary School Journal,* November, 1945.

_____, "Better Teacher Education," *The Elementary School Journal,* November, 1946.

_____ and Corey, Stephen M., "Group Counseling with Teachers," *Educational Administration and Supervision,* September, 1944.

_____, "Curriculum of the Elementary School in the Post-War Period," *National Elementary Principal,* April, 1945.

_____, "Criteria for Appraising Procedures Used to Promote Reading Development, I," *The Elementary School Journal,* December, 1945; "II," January, 1946.

_____, "What Makes a Good Workshop?" *Childhood Education,* May, 1946.

_____, "Measure for Measure," *See and Hear,* May, 1946.

_____, "The Principal Looks at Himself," *Educational Leadership,* April, 1947.

_____, "Effective Leadership Is Duty of Principal," *School Management,* April, 1947.

_____, "Planned and Unplanned Curriculums," *The Elementary School Journal,* June, 1947.

_____, "Toward Better Film Edition," *See and Hear,* October, 1947.

_____, "The Development of International Understanding in The Elementary School," *The Elementary School Journal,* December, 1947.

_____, "The Survey Versus the Cooperative Study," *Educational Administration and Supervision,* Vol. 34, 1948.

_____, "The Conceptual Orientation of a Cooperative Study," *The Elementary School Journal,* February, 1949.

_____ and Zimmermann, Elizabeth, "A Child Study Program: One Phase of a Cooperative Study," *Educational Administration and Supervision,* April, 1949.

_____ and Leary, Bernice, *Putting What We Know About Children's Language Development Into Home and School Practice.* Appeared in National Council of English Teachers Monograph on *Child Development and the Language Arts,* June, 1953. Also appeared in *Elementary English,* April, 1953.

_____, *Recent Trends in Reading.* Speech before International Council for the Improvement of Reading Instruction, Atlantic City, February, 1953; also an article in *The Reading Teacher,* March, 1953.

_____ and Howell, Miriam E., "Growth in Children's Vocabulary," *The Elementary School Journal*, January, 1954.

_____, "Recent Developments in Action Research," *Educational Leadership*, October, 1953.

_____, "Recent Books in Curriculum," *The Elementary School Journal*, December, 1953.

_____, "Approaches to Helping Teachers Improve Their Instructional Practices," *School Review*, December, 1954.

_____, "A Review of the Concept of the Emerging Self," *Teachers' College Record*, February, 1955.

_____, "Curriculum Research," *Educational Leadership*, May, 1955.

_____, "The Future of Teacher Education," *Teachers' College Record*, February, 1956.

_____, "Curriculum Research," *Educational Leadership*, April, 1956.

_____, "Ways for the Superintendent to Improve Program of Inservice Education," *Superintendents Newsletter*, N.E.A., February, 1956.

_____, "The Teacher Looks at the Evaluation Process," *Professional Growth Series*, E. B. Croft, April, 1957.

_____ and Harris, Theodore L., "Exploratory Studies in Perception," *School Life*, Journal of U.S. Office of Education, January, 1958.

_____ and Estvan, Frank J., "Curriculum Research," *Educational Leadership*, December, 1956.

_____, "Problems of Research in Curriculum Design," *Proceedings of AERA*, February, 1957.

_____, "Educational Objectives and Evaluation," *Commission on Instruction*, N.E.A., May, 1959.

_____, "Cooperative Procedures in Learning," *Teachers College Record*, January, 1953.

_____, "Curriculum Decisions and Provisions for Individual Differences," *The Elementary School Journal*, January, 1962.

_____ and Erlebacher, Adrienne, "Quality of Handwriting Today and Yesterday," *The Elementary School Journal*, November, 1961.

_____, "The Sources of Curriculum Planning," *Educational Leadership*, April, 1962.

_____, "The Teaching of Handwriting," *Encyclopedia Britannica* (senior), 1962.

_____, "The Teaching of Handwriting," *The Tennessee Elementary Principal*, November, 1960.

_____, "Manuscript and Cursive Writing," *Childhood Education*, February, 1961.

_____, "What Instrument Should Children Use in Program of Writing Instruction," *National Education Association Journal*, February, 1961.

_____ and Otto, Wayne, "Pressure Patterns in Handwriting," *Journal of Experimental Education*, January, 1962.

_____, "The Ungraded Elementary School," *Harvard Educational Review*, Spring Issue, 1962.

_____, co-director and editor, *Survey of Highland Park Elementary Schools, Districts 107 and 108*. Chicago: University of Chicago Press, 1944.

_____, co-director and editor, *Survey of Barrington Elementary Schools*, Chicago: University of Chicago Press, 1945.

_____, co-director and editor, *Survey of Battle Creek, Michigan, Public School System*. Chicago: University of Chicago Press, 1945.

_____, co-director and editor, *Survey of Oak Park Elementary Schools, District 97*. Chicago: University of Chicago Press, 1946.

_____, *Survey of Milwaukee Country Day School*. Chicago: University of Chicago Press, 1947.

_____ and Wakefield, Howard, *Survey of Educational Program and Building Needs, Milwaukee Downer Seminary*. Wisconsin School Services, 1959.

_____ et al., *Program of Elementary Education in Chicago Public Schools*. School Board, City of Chicago, 1959, 65 pp.

_____, *Survey of Educational Research*. Madison, Wisconsin: Department of Education, University of Wisconsin, 1961–62, November, 1961.

_____ and Otto, W., "Pressure on Point and Banel of a Writing Instrument," *Journal of Experimental Education*, 30 (December, 1961), 215–30.

_____, "Handwriting and Children's Writing," *Elementary English*, 37, February 1961, 264–67.

_____, "Administrative Structure and Processes in Curriculum Development," *Review of Educational Research*, 30 (June, 1960), 258–74.

_____, "Writing Tools for Children," *National Education Association Journal*, 50 (February, 1961), 48–50.